PRAISE FOR *THE ELEPHANT*

'A beautiful book – not just heartwarming but heart healing.' **Chris Riddell**

'A little book with a huge heart.' **Karen Foxlee**

'Carnavas takes the tough topic of caregiver depression and gives it a delicate, graceful touch. His plot weaves tightly together, and the ending twist is a lovely completion. Black-and-white spot illustrations throughout give a visually accessible feel, as do the short chapters ... A delicate, lovely story about caregiver depression that will validate and empower readers.' ***Kirkus Reviews***

'A warm-hearted book of emotional learning, creative problem-solving, and genuine care for others. Recommended for anyone in need of hope for a path to happiness.' ***School Library Journal***

'Sprinkled with humour and endearing illustrations, *The Elephant* is a must read. It will not rip your heart in two with unchecked tragedy. It will, however, massage it firmly and then fill it with gladness. I can't love this enough.' **Boomerang Books**

'A gentle, whimsical and deeply affecting story.' ***Magpies***

PRAISE FOR *MY BROTHER BEN*

'For everyone whose brother is a hero, even if they don't know it yet.' **Morris Gleitzman**

'There should be more books like this: gentle books that draw us slowly in and make us want to linger, books fashioned with kindness and family at their heart. *My Brother Ben* made me remember, and long for, times that were simpler. Well done, Peter Carnavas, and thank you.' **Glenda Millard**

'If you've ever had – or been, or known! – a brother, the ebbs and flows of their relationship will ring absolutely true and linger long past their story's end. *My Brother Ben* is absolutely bursting with heart, and with the kind of quiet power of the very best books, the ones that leave an indelible mark. I didn't know I needed a book about brothers, birds and boats; now I wonder how I was ever without it. Please give *My Brother Ben* to all the boys in your life, and all the girls too.' **Meg McKinlay**

'This story about birdwatching, being different and the bond between brothers is told in Peter's lovely gentle way and it's a real treat. Kids will love it.' **Karen Foxlee**

My Brother Ben

Peter Carnavas

UQP

For my brothers

PROLOGUE

A Strange Feathered Thing

Last year, I found a dead bird on the road outside our house. A young magpie, grey and white. It lay flat with its head on the side, one wing stretched out and the other squashed under its own body. I crouched down, hugged my knees to my chest and stared. Wind tickled the tiny feathers on the bird's breast, its legs stuck out like black twigs and the back of its neck glowed pink in the setting sun.

The bitumen warmed my feet, but my body shivered. Cold, but also scared: a bird had been thumped by a car, knocked out of the air, when all it had wanted to do was fly. Now it lay dead on the road and the only person around was me. I stretched my fingers towards it, but pulled back. My hand shook and I swallowed hard. I reached again and my fingers brushed its feathers. Then a dark shape was suddenly behind me, getting bigger, roaring closer.

I jumped too late and the car punched my side. Threw me off the road. I hit the ground and rolled, a mess of arms and legs across the dirt. I choked and coughed, trying to suck air back in. Somebody was on top of me, shaking me, screaming my name.

'Luke!'

It wasn't the car that hit me. It was Ben, tackling me out of the way. The car disappeared around the corner in the fading light.

'Luke!' Ben yelled into my face, shaking my shoulders. 'What were you doing?'

I rolled out from under my brother and sat on the gutter until my breathing slowed down. I squinted and pointed at the magpie. It lay in the same position, unmoved by the rushing car. Ben walked onto the road. He bent down, gathered the bird in his shirt and held it close to his belly. But he didn't just hold it.

He cradled it, like he was nursing a bowl full of jelly that hadn't set. I caught up to him as he headed home.

'What are you gonna do?' I said.

'Find a box.'

'To bury it?'

Ben stopped, his eyes dark and serious. 'Could be alive.' A streetlight flickered on, lighting the side of his face. 'Trust me.' He always said that.

We found a big cardboard box under the house and set it at the end of the verandah. Stuffed it with too many blankets and rags, and filled an old yoghurt cup with water. As Ben slid the magpie inside, I still didn't know if we had made a nest or a coffin. But the next morning, we padded outside to find the magpie awake, huddled in a corner of the box, testing its voice with a soft gargly song.

'Wonder what it's saying.' My voice cracked with sleep.

'That you've got bad breath,' said Ben, walking back inside.

The thrill of saving a bird's life was over for Ben, but not for me. I sat with the magpie on the warm verandah, still in my pyjama shorts. I offered more water in a cup, then I whispered so that only the bird could hear. 'You'd better be more careful crossing the road, buddy. Or at least fly a bit higher.'

It watched me with a chocolate-brown eye and tilted its head, as if it understood. We held the stare for a few seconds before a thought sailed into my mind. I ran to my room, grabbed a book from under my bed and returned to the verandah. I read the title to the magpie. '*Field Guide to Australian Birds*.'

Aunty Gem had given it to me a few weeks earlier, just after Dad left. I'd hardly touched it until now. Inside the front cover was a message in Gem's looped handwriting.

Dear Luke,
Things don't always work out the way we hope they will. But even on the dark days, birds still sing. So open a window and look outside, for when you open your eyes to birds, the world opens itself in return.
Love Gem.

I didn't really know what it meant, but I liked the way it sounded. I watched the magpie beside me and tried to open my eyes a bit more, like Gem had written. Its beak was sharpened to a dark point, thin feathery trousers grew halfway down its legs, and one scaly toe was bent. Then I found the page of magpies in the book. It was beautiful. I ran my fingers over the coloured illustrations and read words I'd never even heard before. Plumage. Underwings. Fledgling. Bird words, wonderful and strange. As the verandah boards grew hotter under my legs, I learnt everything there was to know about magpies.

For the next few days, I sat beside the box and watched over the bird. It didn't take any of the bugs and worms I offered, but it drank lots of water. Along the way, it woke up enough to perch on the box and bounce onto the railing. Sometimes I read pages from the bird guide out loud and the magpie turned its head at the sound of my voice.

One morning, Ben wandered from the kitchen, scooping cereal from a bowl.

Australian magpie

‘You still here?’ He laughed. I didn’t know if he was talking to me or the bird. Then his face softened when he saw mine. ‘What are you so happy about?’

I hadn’t felt the smile on my face, but I knew it had something to do with the magpie and Gem’s words – my eyes opening and the world opening up in return. I’d stopped thinking about Dad and had focused on the bird, this strange feathered thing reborn in a cardboard box on our verandah. I wanted to know more: all things about all birds.

Ben nodded at the magpie as it scratched under a wing with its beak. ‘You should give it a name.’

I smiled. Somehow I knew it was a girl. ‘It’s not that original, but … Maggie?’

Ben tipped his bowl and slurped the last bit of milk. ‘Cool.’

As soon as I’d named her, Maggie hopped from the box and landed on my shoulder. I ducked and laughed, then relaxed. I stroked the feathers on her chest and she tilted her head. I thought of her lying still on the road a few days before, and I re-read Gem’s message in the front of the book: *Things don't always work out.* It was true. Parents don't always stick around. Birds get knocked out of the sky. But this was my chance to make one of those things right.

'I'll stick with you,' I said to Maggie. I wasn't worried about Ben hearing me. 'Trust me.'

As I said his favourite words, it felt like I was in charge of something. The kind of feeling Ben probably had all the time.

A moment later, Maggie leapt off my shoulder and landed on the railing. She shook her feathers and tested her wings with a few flightless beats. Then she flapped a wobbly path to a branch in the poinciana tree, right outside our bedroom. She threw back her head and sang a song to the bright summer sky. Happy, like me, to still be alive, thanks to my brother Ben.

CHAPTER 1

The Jumping Tree

We sat in the boat, facing each other. I gripped the side and a piece of white paint flaked off under my fingernail. Ben lay back, put his hands behind his head and closed his eyes. 'This is it, Lukey. A life on the water.'

I lay back too and rested my head on the rough wooden edge. Water lapped nearby and Maggie sang from a tall tree. Nearly a year after we'd found her, she was still with us. Scratching around the verandah, keeping watch from the roof and singing outside our bedroom almost every morning.

'Where should we go?' Ben said.

I closed my eyes, just like him. Imagined the water rocking me along, taking me anywhere I wanted. 'Let's go and find that eagle's nest.'

'The big one?'

'Yep. White-bellied sea eagle.'

We lay like that for a while. Ben whistled a lazy tune. A few swamphens honked to each other, far away.

Then Maggie squawked and Ben jolted up. 'Quick! Someone's coming.'

We grabbed our stuff – his shirt, my sketchbook – and jumped out of the boat, landing hard on the ground. We hadn't really been on the water. It wasn't even our boat. Just an old dinghy tied to a tree in someone's backyard. A man's voice yelled and we sprinted out of the yard, through the bush and down to the creek. Our feet slapped along the muddy bank. We dodged mangrove shoots and dipped under branches. Climbed over rocks, kicked through scrub and didn't stop until we reached the Jumping Tree.

We collapsed on the ground and caught our breath. Ben's feet were cut up and I had scratches all over my legs. He walked ankle-deep into the saltwater to soak his feet. We were both hurting and puffed, but my head tingled with the excitement of it all.

'Who was that guy?' I said. 'Did you see him?'

'Dunno.' He lifted a foot to inspect the cuts. 'Good job keeping up for once.'

'Me? I was faster than you.'

He smiled. We both knew it wasn't true.

I sat on the bank and brushed dirt off my hands. 'Lucky we didn't get caught, though.' It was the last thing Mum needed, us getting in trouble. She was already working till dark and doing everything herself.

'He was never gonna catch us,' said Ben. 'No-one knows the creek like us.'

'You mean, no-one knows *the edge* of the creek like us.'

Everyone with a boat knew the rest of it: the deep channels and secret inlets. And even though we all called it a creek, it was much bigger. More like a cross between a river and a lake, a band of salty brown water that snaked behind the houses and breathed up and down with the tides. Some parts were narrow enough to throw a rock to the other side, but most of it was wide like the school oval.

I opened my sketchbook and made a few pencil marks in the shape of a heron. Ben started to climb the Jumping Tree, a huge paperbark that stood like a twisted giant among the mangroves and clumps of spiny grass. He clawed his way up the trunk, then crab-walked along the thick branch that hung over the water. Maggie sat on a higher arm of the tree and cocked her head.

'Don't worry, Maggie,' I said. 'He's just showing off.'

She gargled back.

Ben stood on the end of the branch, ready to jump. I stopped drawing and looked up. A white-headed pigeon cut across the sky and the rattling song of cicadas swelled around us like a drumroll. Ben closed his eyes and stretched his arms wide, as if it all belonged to him: the trees, the creek, the disappearing pigeon. He puffed his chest, then jumped.

For a moment, his arms were like wings. The air held him up. He was a king parrot, a dancing brolga, a wedge-tailed eagle taking flight. For that second he was in the air, everything else

seemed to stop. The birds stopped singing, insects fell quiet, the creek lay still. Then he crashed into the water and the world clicked back into gear. Maggie and the other birds lifted to the sky. Colour seeped back into branches and leaves. And the creek woke up as Ben's splash sent circles rippling to the banks.

He rocketed back up through the surface. 'Come in, Lukey!'

I never jumped from the tree, but there was another way in. A length of rope was tied to the branch, and we kept the end coiled to a stumpy shoot that stuck out from the trunk. I dropped my sketchbook and unwound the rope, then gripped it like a vine. I pushed off from the muddy bank, swung out over the creek and let go. The cool water swallowed me and I sank until my toes dipped into the mud at the bottom. Then I rose up, floated on my back and watched the paperbark leaves dance against the sky. Ben did the same. We were two sea stars spinning slowly on the surface.

CHAPTER 2

The Boat

We started to walk home from the Jumping Tree. Ben once worked out it was a forty-minute hike – as long as a maths lesson but with a lot less yawning. Grey mud squelched between our toes as we went, and sandflies buzzed around our legs. Maggie came and went, darting off on bird business, then reappearing on branches ahead of us. We stepped out of the mud and scuffed along the dirt path that ran beside the creek. Sometimes it was jungle-thick, other times the trees were spread out and we saw houses in between the trunks and branches. They were all old

Queenslander houses like ours, wooden boxes on tall stilts, with wide verandahs and stairs at the front and back. Not many people had fences, so the yards joined up with the bush. I could've chucked a cricket ball from most back doors and landed it in the water. Ben could have cleared the whole creek.

It wasn't long until we spotted the boat again, tied to the tree like a forgotten pet.

'What would you do, Lukey? Where would you go first?'

I knew what he was talking about. All the time we'd lived on the creek, we'd never had a boat.

'I'd follow that bird,' I said, as a kingfisher swooped to the other side. 'I reckon there's loads more over there.'

I didn't ask him. I knew he'd tell me.

'I'd go exploring. Follow the creek as far as it goes.' He turned and looked at the water, like he was picturing himself there. 'Can you imagine? Just being able to take off? Catch fish. Camp wherever. Sleep in the boat during the day.'

I closed my eyes and saw it all. Snoozing in the boat, pulling a fat whiting out of the water for dinner. It was Ben's dream – not mine – but I'd follow him anywhere.

'The first place I'd go would be The Pocket,' he said.

Ben was always talking about The Pocket, a passage of deep water that was home to the biggest fish in the creek. We'd never been there but every other kid in the world had, because every other kid had a boat. Even Dad had talked about it: adventures from his childhood we wished were ours. Now it seemed so far away and all we had were secondhand stories.

'I heard Emily in Grade Six caught ten bream in a row,' I said. 'All keepers.'

'And Jason Singh caught a flathead a metre long, he reckons.' Ben measured a rough metre between his hands. 'Imagine that – a metre!'

Then Maggie sang, waking us from our thoughts, and we kept pushing along the track. On the way, we passed a girl about Ben's age. She wore a floppy hat and held a long crooked stick like a hiking pole. After she'd passed, Ben stood as still as a fence post and gazed at her until she was gone.

I threw a twig at his head. 'You okay?'

'Yeah. Why?'

'Thought you were gonna blow her a kiss.'

He glared at me. 'You're dead.'

I laughed and bolted along the path and he chased me home.

CHAPTER 3

Bird Calls

Our backyard was all dirt and patchy grass, a chook pen on one side, clothesline on the other. A few rotted posts marked where a fence once stood, but now the yard just rolled into Cabbage Tree Creek. A wonky wooden jetty reached from the bank into the water, and the surrounding scrub reminded us we were on the outskirts of town. Hardly any kids lived near our place and that was why it was usually just the two of us. Most people were clumped in houses closer to school and the main street of shops. That was a half-hour bike ride away, less with the wind behind me.

I sat facing the creek with my back to the house. Mum would still be working, typing articles on her laptop until night. I opened my sketchbook and started drawing a kingfisher. Ben stepped into a handstand.

'Not long to go,' I said.

'Huh?' Ben walked on his hands for a few seconds, then pushed himself to land back on his feet. 'Till what?'

'School,' I said. 'Remember school?'

'Oh.' He scratched the back of his neck. 'Hadn't thought about it.'

I shook my head. 'You hadn't thought about starting high school?'

He looked at me with those dark eyes. People said we were similar, and we sort of were, except he had everything in the right place, the right size. At twelve, he already had proper muscles. Two years younger, I was all skinny arms and big ears.

'Don't wanna think about it,' he said. He faced the water, stared back the way we'd come. Probably thinking about escaping in a boat. 'What about you, little Lukey?' He put on a pretend baby

voice. 'Will you be okay without big Ben to look after you?'

I laughed. 'Are you serious? No-one stealing my lunch? Can't wait.'

But I wasn't looking forward to it. I tried to picture myself in the covered area at school without Ben and his mates around. He was always there, in the corner of my eye, but in the middle of everything, like the sun surrounded by all the planets.

He sat beside me and pulled at some grass. 'You ever gonna jump out of the tree? It's like flying, you know.'

I shrugged and scribbled some shading on my kingfisher, but made a mess of it. Jumping out of trees was a Ben thing to do.

'What are you scared of?' he said.

'That my face'll hit the water too hard and I'll end up looking like you.'

He laughed and pushed me over, rubbed my head in the grass. He let go and we both sat up. It took me a while to stop giggling.

He folded his hands behind his head and lay back on the grass. I did the same. As I listened to the birds throw their songs across the creek,

I thought of their names. Butcherbird. Corella. Dusky moorhen.

Ben flashed me a look. 'Go on, then,' he said. 'What can you hear?'

This was my thing, what Mum called my party trick. Ben could jump out of trees, climb on the roof, kick a ball into the next neighbourhood. But this was mine. A Luke thing to do.

The first one was easy. A pretty, warbling song.

'That's Maggie,' I said.

Next, a thin, high-pitched whistle. Just one note.

'King parrot.'

Tiny chirping.

'Red-backed fairy-wren.'

I closed my eyes and drifted into the birdsong, heard nothing but whistles, trills and squeaks. The calls swam around me, overlapped and answered each other. I named them all. Robins, wrens and wagtails. Ducks, doves and lorikeets. I even caught the distant squeal of a whistling kite.

Then something strange. A scratchy call, a sort of squeak. Like a parrot, but nothing I'd heard before. I opened my eyes. There it was again. A soft, chirpy squeak.

'I don't know that one.'

Ben stood, brushed the grass off his shorts, then grabbed my hand and pulled me up. 'Must be a new bird in town.'

CHAPTER 4

Happy Family

We tumbled up the back stairs to the verandah, which was the best part of our house. It was bigger than any of the rooms inside and stood high enough for me to see everything: the creek, the neighbours' rooftops, gum trees waving from the end of the block. There was another set of steps at the front door, and the house was a grid of small square rooms, three of them bedrooms. One for Mum, another for her work, and one for Ben and me.

We thumped into the kitchen as Mum wandered out of her study. Her face was tired, but she switched on some old music and shuffled around the kitchen in her socks. 'Leftover spaghetti?'

I nodded and Ben gave her a thumbs-up as he guzzled a glass of milk.

She plonked the bowls on the table. I twirled the spaghetti around my fork to make a pasta whirlpool. Ben shovelled his down.

'Did you go far today?' She clipped her hair back and picked up a fork.

'Jumping Tree,' said Ben, between mouthfuls.

Mum looked at me sideways, eyebrows arched. 'Any new birds?'

I shook my head. Hadn't seen a new one for ages. 'I heard something, though. A bird call I didn't know.'

'There's no such thing, is there?'

I grinned and sipped some water. 'Also, Ben fell in love.'

He scowled and pointed a butter knife at me. 'Dare you to say it again.'

'Enough, you two.' Mum twisted some pepper into her bowl. 'Your dad's going to ring tomorrow, at twelve o'clock.'

Ben nodded. I concentrated on the spaghetti.

'Luke?'

Dad had been calling for nearly a year and I never talked to him. At first, Mum didn't care. She was too busy doing weird things after he left. She dyed her hair, bought a new couch and baked cakes almost every day. I wondered if she was trying to flush out any last trace of Dad with the smell of muffins. Then she found a website that gave her some new ideas. She stopped baking, started yoga and nagged us to talk to Dad. Ben did, but I couldn't do it.

'I'm going birdwatching with Gem tomorrow.' My usual excuse. I kept my eyes down, but she didn't pester me. Just sighed and squeezed my hand.

'Hey, Mum.' Ben poked his spaghetti with his fork. 'Do you know who owns that white boat?'

She faced him. They had the same dark eyes. 'Where is it?'

'Tied up in someone's backyard not far from the Jumping Tree. It hasn't been there long.'

'Not sure. A few people have moved in lately.'

Ben dragged spaghetti strands around the bowl. 'Well, whoever they are, they're idiots.'

'Ben, don't talk like—'

'Sorry, but who would leave a boat tied up all the time and never use it? It's cruel. To us *and* the boat.'

Mum tilted her head and her mouth curved into a half-smile. She could say everything with that smile – that she knew he wanted a boat and that it wasn't fair other people didn't use theirs.

He shoved the fork into his mouth and more spaghetti disappeared, like in those movies where a monster gulps a fistful of people in one go. He leant back and we followed his gaze to watch a gecko catch a moth on the ceiling.

Later, I lay on my bed, reading the bird guide Aunty Gem had given me. After that first morning with Maggie, I carried this book everywhere. The lure of birds pulled me outside, opened my eyes and dragged me clear of the Dad-shaped shadow he'd left behind. Best of all, I discovered I was good at spotting birds and remembering their names. I knew the difference between a whistler and a warbler. Could identify an eagle by the shape of its tail. I knew that catbirds had red eyes, weebills were only nine centimetres long and that a grey fantail's nest was shaped like a wineglass.

I flicked through the book. The pages were dirty, the spine broken and the whole thing was buckled and stained from the time I dropped it in the creek.

Ben started doing sit-ups, his feet hooked under the metal frame of his bed, then he spotted the guide in my hands. 'Read some out.' His voice strained. 'Some good ones.'

They were all good ones. Flycatchers, nightjars and chats. Treecreepers, logrunners, curlews. I loved them all. But I knew what he meant. He wanted to hear about the weird ones. The funny ones.

'The barking owl sounds like someone screaming.'

'Scary,' he said, puffed.

I turned a few pages.

'White-winged choughs kidnap chicks from each other.'

'That sucks.'

'Look at this one,' I said, tapping the page.

He grunted on his last sit-up, then rolled

over and sat on my bed. 'Ugly. What is it?'

'Apostlebird,' I said. 'But they get called happy family birds.'

'Why?'

I zigzagged my finger down the page. 'Here – because they stick together, like a family.'

Ben lay back, stretching his arms behind his head. He looked up at the ceiling. 'That's you and me,' he said. 'Happy family birds.'

I lay back too, with my arms like his. 'Because we stick together?'

'Nah,' he said. 'Because we're ugly.'

We both cracked up laughing. I tumbled around, losing my breath. The book fell off the bed.

After a while, Mum hugged us goodnight and we switched off the light. I looked out the window at the charcoal sky. Somewhere a tawny frogmouth hooted. I heard Ben turn over in his bed.

'Hey, Luke.' He whispered, but it sounded loud in the dark. 'You can come, you know.'

'Where?'

'Exploring. In the boat, I mean. If we get one.'

I sat up. 'Where would we go?'

'I got it all worked out. We'd take off from our jetty, head straight across to the other side. You can find that bird you saw today and all its friends. Then we'd go south, away from the Jumping Tree, all the way past that old windmill. You know?'

'Where that dead tree sticks out of the water?'

'That's it. Follow that bend to The Pocket. We'd fish all day, catch flathead and bream.'

'How many?'

'A whole bucketful. We'd camp on the bank and cook the fish and fall asleep under the stars.'

'And the birds would wake us up in the morning.'

'Yep. There'd be no-one else around. Just us and the birds.'

He stopped talking then. I lay back down and closed my eyes, imagined myself asleep in a boat.

CHAPTER 5

Aunty Gem

The next day, I bumped about in the passenger seat of Aunty Gem's old ute. It rattled and shook around every corner and Gem sang along to the radio at the top of her voice. Chocolate wrappers and empty drink bottles tumbled around my feet. A line of little plastic bird toys were stuck to the dashboard, like a small army of feathered warriors facing the road.

Aunty Gem was Mum's younger sister. She didn't have any kids and Mum said that was why she was louder and funnier. Less to worry about. She was the only person I knew who loved birds more than I did. After I'd found

Maggie, and Gem saw me carrying the bird guide around, she started taking me to her favourite birding spots. Lagoons, forests and even a specially built bird hide on our creek. Then she came over every weekend to teach me bird calls. Bird by bird, she played their voices on her phone and I named them.

Four-note, rhythmic squawk.

'Rainbow pitta.'

A low, muffled grunt.

'Topknot pigeon.'

Rising note and a sharp crack.

'Easy. Eastern whipbird.'

By the end of the year I could pick almost every one, especially the birds that lived close.

She taught me other things too. How to be quiet and patient, and how to pick a spot and wait for birds to come to me. I learnt to be still and wait for movement. My senses grew keen. There were more colours around me, more sounds, and it all reminded me of Gem's message: *when you open your eyes to birds, the world opens itself in return.* But there was another side to birdwatching that had nothing to do with birds.

'It helps you tune out,' she said once. 'When you sit by a pond, trying to glimpse a grebe or a pygmy-goose, you forget about whatever gets you down.'

One day I asked her what the birds helped her to forget.

'Boring grown-up stuff. Remember that girlfriend I had, the vet nurse?'

I shook my head.

'Good.' She squawked a laugh. 'Neither do I.'

A few songs later, the ute chugged to a stop on a stretch of grass, across the other side of the suburb. We hopped out and left the toy birds keeping watch from the dash. I looped my binoculars round my neck and we stood on the platform overlooking the wetlands, one of our favourite spots.

'What do you see, Lukey Luke?' She looked a bit like a bird herself, a kind of cockatoo with a funky crest of dark red hair.

'Jacana,' I said straightaway, pointing to the strange long-toed birds prancing on the lily pads. 'A cormorant, some pelicans, a few wood

ducks. There's a tern flying above the little island out there.'

Gem peered through her binoculars, more powerful than mine. I was always itching to look through those lenses. 'You're right. A whiskered tern.'

It went on, the two of us swinging our heads around, binoculars glued to our eyes. We spoke our secret language of bird names. Godwits and swallows. Whistlers and grebes. My favourite was the double-barred finch, a tiny round bird with an owl-like face, not much bigger than the birds on the dashboard.

A few hours later, we were back in the ute, bouncing our way home. Gem rocked along to an old song about dancing on a Saturday night and I smiled at my suburb as it passed by the car window: a couple waited at the train station, a family rode bikes along the footpath and a grey-haired man latched the bakery door, closing up for the day. Everything sparkled, the way it always did after I'd been watching birds with Gem.

CHAPTER 6

An Unexpected Gift

My birthday arrived a few days later, near the end of January. A pedestal fan buzzed in the corner of the lounge room as everybody watched me open my presents: a tin of sketching pencils, a new sleeping bag and a book about a man who tried to see all the birds in Australia. Then Aunty Gem handed me a small package with a card that said 'Happy Bird-day'. I unwrapped it and held in my hands a familiar pair of binoculars. I turned them over and ran my finger along the smooth edges and the brown leather strap.

'But aren't these yours?' I said.

Her face was all shiny. 'Not anymore. I want you to have them.'

I held the lenses up to my eyes. They felt at home in my hands. 'Thanks.'

'What about this one?' Ben tapped a present wrapped in brown paper. 'From Dad.'

A year earlier, Dad was here for my birthday. He sang and ate cake like everything was normal, but the next day, he told us he was moving out, all the way to Perth. I hated thinking about it because when he hugged me on my birthday, he must have been planning it all, working out what to say the next day. He thought he was doing the right thing, but it just made me mad.

I frowned at the present. 'I don't want it.'

Mum slid off the couch and squeezed me in a hug. 'Maybe later, hey?'

Ben peeled himself off the beanbag. 'Time for *my* present, then.'

He threw an arm over my shoulder and handed me something small, squashed and wrapped in newspaper. I ripped it open and found a half-eaten peanut butter sandwich.

'Couldn't finish it this morning,' he said, patting my back, 'so I thought you might like it.'

'Wow, thanks.'

I stuffed the sandwich down the back of his shirt and bolted. He chased me through the kitchen, onto the verandah and down the stairs, waving the sandwich above his head.

'It's your present!' He laughed. 'Don't you want it?'

I sprinted down the backyard to the creek and he caught me as we hit the water. We tackled and wrestled, then he scooped me up and dragged me to the bank. I fell on the mud and laughed. Saltwater snorted out of my nose.

He looked at the backyard. 'I dropped the sandwich somewhere.'

I tapped him on the arm and pointed to the top of a gum tree. Maggie peered at us from a high branch with the sandwich clamped in her beak.

'You can have it!' I called, though she probably wouldn't eat it.

Ben grabbed my hand and pulled me up. 'Shame. It was a good sandwich.'

I gave him a shove. As we walked back to the house, he rested his elbow on top of my head.

Back in the lounge room, Mum was beaming.

'Just spotted this!' She waved Ben's newspaper wrapping in front of us.

I took it and scanned the writing.

'It's a competition,' I said, then turned to Ben. 'To win a boat.'

CHAPTER 7

Community Pride

We sat on the back steps and studied the page like it was the most important document in the world. The competition was being run by the local council, just for kids under fifteen. You had to make something that celebrated Cabbage Tree Creek. A painting, a story, photographs – anything that showed off the creek. The article said it was about 'instilling community pride', but the most important detail was the first prize: a three-metre fishing canoe, with paddles, life jackets and the chance to name the boat. They'd paint the name on the side for you.

'This is it, Lukey,' said Ben, leaping up and dancing on the steps like they were hot coals. 'This is our boat. We have to win it.'

I read the page over and over. Something to celebrate the creek. Community pride. I had no idea what to do. Ben bounced on his toes, whispering a made-up song about a boat. Maggie stalked around the grass at the bottom of the steps, tilting her head to listen for wriggles in the dirt.

'You hungry, Mag?' I said.

She gurgled back.

Another bird sang a beautiful flute-like call that rang out across the neighbourhood.

'What was that?' Ben said, turning to the sound.

'Pied butcherbird,' I said. My favourite bird call.

Ben stopped dancing. He grinned at me, his eyes wide. 'That's it!'

'What?'

'Birds, Lukey. Birds! You could make a list of all the birds in the creek. No-one knows birds like you do.'

I shook my head and laughed, but my heart hit a bit harder in my chest. This was something I could do. Something Ben thought I could do.

'I could draw them,' I said.

'Yes!' Ben was really dancing now, swinging his hips and clicking his fingers. 'This is it! This is it! We can make a book.'

'We could call it *The Birds of Cabbage Tree Creek.*'

Ben cheered and ran down the steps. He danced around the yard, singing 'Row, Row, Row Your Boat'. I looked at the creek, pictured us there in the canoe. We'd each have a paddle, fishing lines dragging behind us. No-one else around. Just us and the birds.

CHAPTER 8

A Shiny Bream

The morning after my birthday, I woke early and took my sketchbook to the verandah. I opened to a blank page and tapped my finger on the point of a sharpened pencil, ready to draw the first entry for *The Birds of Cabbage Tree Creek*.

'Come on, then,' I said to Maggie as she strutted along the railing. 'Keep still so I can draw.'

She spun, showing me her other side, as if she were parading down a fashion runway.

'Do you want to be first in the book or not?'

She peered at me for a second, then stood in a perfect side-on pose.

'Thanks.' I made a rough outline that I could finish later.

After breakfast, Ben rigged up his fishing rod, I stuffed my binoculars and sketchbook into a bag and we set off to find as many birds as we could. Before we reached the track beside the creek, we spotted a handful of regulars in the yard – rainbow lorikeets, grey butcherbirds and noisy miners. A willie wagtail followed us for a while, spinning and bouncing between branches. Then some ducks, a fantail, an egret, and pretty soon we had over ten birds on the list.

We passed the other backyards that rolled into the creek and, after a while, we stopped near the white boat.

'Imagine if we took it,' Ben joked. 'We could get it to the water before they noticed. Paddle away and they'd still be snoring in front of the TV.' He closed his eyes and pretended to snore.

'Come on,' I laughed. 'Let's keep going.'

At the Jumping Tree, we left our gear on the

dirt. Ben climbed the tree and flung himself off the branch. I swung out on the rope and dropped into the water. We cooled off and dreamt up adventures we'd have in the boat, paddling all the way to the mouth of the creek where it spilt into the bay.

A white-bellied sea eagle soared above us.

'It's so still,' said Ben. 'Like I'm looking at a photo.'

We climbed out of the water and he picked up his rod. He threaded a worm onto the hook and cast the line. The reel whirred as the bait sailed over the surface then landed with a gentle plop. Ben stood as still as a dead branch, the rod resting easily in his hand like it was a part of him, an extra limb.

I shook the water from my hair. A strange bird call floated on the wind. It was the same scratchy song, that soft squeak I'd heard before. Some kind of parrot, or rosella. I scanned the scrub with the binoculars.

'I gotta find it,' I whispered.

'What?'

'That bird.'

white-bellied sea eagle

Ben tilted his head to listen. 'Can't hear it.'

'You probably whacked your head on a branch when you jumped out of the tree.'

'I'll whack *your* head in a minute.'

Suddenly, he whipped the rod back over his shoulder.

'Got it!' He started reeling in. The rod bent, nearly touching the surface, as the winding line cut a rippled path through the water. I crouched on a rock near the edge and spotted the silver shape weave towards us. Ben pulled the fish into the shallows. Then it leapt clear of the water, catching the sunlight on its scales, and landed with a wet slap on the bank. A shiny bream, but not big enough to keep. Ben dropped the rod and slipped the hook from the fish's lip, avoiding the spikes on its back. He eased it back into the creek.

'They'll be bigger at The Pocket.' He wiped his hands on his wet shorts. 'Trust me.'

We did the same for the rest of the week. Wandered the banks of the creek, scribbled down birds and threw ourselves in the water. Sometimes a boat passed by, slicing through the surface, sending a roll of ankle-high waves towards the banks. As each one disappeared around a bend, we imagined new adventures for ourselves. Dreamt of secret waterways and untouched islands, places just for us.

One afternoon, the girl with the floppy hat strode along the track with a fishing rod and net. Ben stuck his chest out, said hi, and they talked for a while. I tried to concentrate on the golden whistler in my sketchbook, but I heard a few things. Her name was Frankie, she lived with her dad, and she was starting at the same high school as Ben.

When she was gone, he sat on a fallen tree and stared at the other side for a long time. 'Ever noticed how many different greens you can see in the one tree?'

I thought about our week of finding birds and remembered Aunty Gem's words. *When you open your eyes to birds, the world opens itself in return.* Maybe that was happening to Ben. Or maybe the floppy-hat girl had turned his brain to mud.

CHAPTER 9

A Hole in the Sky

One night near the end of the holidays, we camped in the backyard to look for night birds. Whenever we pitched the tent, Mum timed us.

'Ready, boys,' she said, eyes on her phone's stopwatch. 'Go!'

Ben shook the tent from the bag and I unrolled it across the grass. It was a small tent with poles that crisscrossed through slots in the roof, then curved to make a dome. First, we spread out the tent and stretched it into a tight square. I stuck pegs in each corner and Ben followed me, smacking each one into the ground with a mallet. We threaded the poles through the slots, then lifted the whole thing into its arched shape. Last, we threw the rain cover on top, hammered in a few more pegs and tightened all the ropes.

'Done!'

Mum tapped her phone. 'Two minutes and eleven seconds!'

'That's a record.' Ben laughed. We high-fived.

'Have a good night,' said Mum. 'And come get me if you need anything.' She went upstairs to where Aunty Gem was waiting with the Scrabble board.

The sky turned from blue to milky grey. The moon sailed slowly over the treetops, the colour of custard. It looked so big this early in the evening.

'What do you reckon it looks like?' I threw my sleeping bag and pillow into the tent. 'Sometimes I imagine it's a hole in the sky, like a window to somewhere else.'

Ben crossed his arms and looked up. 'Looks like a biscuit. Or maybe I'm just hungry.'

We scoffed a couple of sandwiches, then wandered to the creek. The moon had drifted behind some clouds and we held our torches like small weapons against the dark. A breeze prickled my skin.

'Hear anything?' Ben swung his torchlight from tree to tree, like he was trying to spot a criminal on the loose.

'Not yet.'

'What about now?'

'No.'

'Now?'

'Shut up.'

'You shut up.'

We sat on the cold grass and fell quiet. Even the flying foxes seemed to relax on their branches. The air stilled. I closed my eyes and listened. Cicadas rattled their tuneless songs. Frogs grunted conversations across the creek. Then something else.

'What's that?' Ben said.

A short, low sound cut through the choir of insects and frogs. It was beautiful, like the deep note of a clarinet. It sounded again, this time two notes, the second higher than the first. My hands trembled. I fumbled with the torch. This bird never came to Cabbage Tree Creek.

'What is it?' Ben whispered.

I put my hand on his shoulder. We shone the torches at the trees on the other side, panning the lights across the trunks, searching higher. Suddenly, our torchlights met and landed together on a bird. But it seemed more than a bird. An angry feathered beast.

Ben shook my arm. 'What is that thing?'

A splatter of marks covered its chest like armour. Thick yellow talons dug into the branch. Golden eyes shone like fiery discs in the torchlight. I knew exactly what it was, but I could hardly get the words out.

'That,' I said, catching my breath, 'is a powerful owl.'

And, in a moment, it had gone. Disappeared into the night on silent wings. We ran back to the yard and crawled into the tent. I didn't draw the picture straightaway. Instead we talked all night, told the story again and again, to make sure it had really happened. As if retelling it was the only thing that stopped the whole night from flying silently away.

CHAPTER 10

Brown Thornbill

I told Gem about the owl the next morning as we bobbed along in the ute. We were on our way to a nearby beach, part of the bay that fed the tides of Cabbage Tree Creek.

'I love powerful owls,' she said. 'They're like feathered monsters.'

'It was huge.' The window wobbled as I wound it down and the air smelt like salt. 'Do they really live at our creek?'

'They might, but I've never seen one. Maybe it just wanted to be a part of your book.'

I smiled. 'I can't believe how quickly it

disappeared. One moment it was there and then—'

I stopped as a picture of Dad flashed in my mind. It darkened my words, the way a storm cloud blackens the sky and cuts short a game of backyard cricket. My dad, the powerful owl – here, then gone.

Gem slipped me the same half-smile that Mum had, like she knew what I was thinking. 'He's calling today, isn't he?'

I nodded. 'Ben's probably talking to him right now.'

She rolled her window down and the breeze rushed through the car. It woke the rubbish at my feet and sent a chip packet flipping and spinning like a grey fantail.

'Your mum's worried.' She kept her eyes on the road. 'I love birding with you, Lukey Luke, but I can't whisk you away every time he calls.'

I twisted my fingers in my lap. 'But that's what birds are for – to get my mind off things. That's what you said.'

Her hands were steady on the wheel. 'You're right. But you can't run away from those things forever.'

I crossed my arms to squash the pounding in my chest. 'He started it.' It sounded stupid, but it was true.

At the beach, we walked along the sand. The flat grey water of the bay was almost all we could see. In the distance, a plane followed its nose up into the hazy sky. My head felt heavy from the conversation in the car, but I relaxed when I spotted birds on the beach. They gathered in groups, a bit like everyone at school. Plovers scurried around like little kids in a sandpit. Whimbrels poked the ground, up and down, like they'd been told to pick up rubbish. A silver gull stood alone, away from the rest.

'How many birds have you drawn for your book?' Gem said.

'About twenty so far. But I've heard one and I don't know what it is.'

She pulled her phone from her pocket and played some bird calls. None of them sounded right.

'I know it's something special. What do you

call it when a bird visits from far away and it's not supposed to?'

'A vagrant.'

It was a strange word. I wanted to say it. 'I reckon it's a vagrant. Something that doesn't belong.'

Gem breathed a laugh through her nose. 'A bit like us, then.'

We sat on the sand and she pointed to an osprey as it hunted over the bay. It hung in the air, watching for a flash of silver in the water. Like a school principal, looking for troublemakers.

'What's your soul bird, Luke?'

'Soul bird?'

'Something I just made up. I mean, if you were a bird, what would you be? I'd be a scarlet honeyeater.'

'Because of your hair?'

'Yep. Bright red feathers. And they like to be alone a lot of the time.'

A plane angled towards a runway on the other side of the bay.

'Sometimes I think Ben's a wedge-tailed eagle,' I said. 'Or something fast like a peregrine falcon.'

Gem scruffed my hair. 'But what about *you*, Lukey Luke?'

I scrunched up my face like I was thinking hard. Remembered what Gem had just said, that we were a bit like vagrants. It made sense, but I couldn't say it. A vagrant sounded too exciting.

'Nothing special,' I said. 'Something small and plain, like a brown thornbill.'

She stared at me, eyebrows bunched down like she was trying to work something out. 'You think your brother's a wedgie and you're just a little brown thornbill?'

I nodded. She rocked back and laughed, sounding more like a cockatoo than a scarlet honeyeater. Just before we left, the osprey plunged feet-first into the bay and flew off with a shiny fish in its talons.

CHAPTER 11

A Smile in the Dark

I stood knee-deep in the creek with a tennis ball in my hand. Ben balanced on the edge of the wooden jetty that jutted from our yard. He leant forward, ready to jump. I threw the ball flat and hard, so it flew past the edge of the jetty. Ben launched himself at the ball, flung an arm out to catch it, then hit the water.

'Woohoo!' He sprang back out, holding the ball high. 'What a catch!'

It was the last day of the holidays and we'd been practising classic catches all afternoon. The edge of the jetty was only a metre above the creek's surface, nowhere near as high as the

Jumping Tree. I'd caught most of mine but not as many as Ben.

'Last one, Lukey?'

I ran onto the jetty. The wood was smooth under my feet. I reached the edge and bent forward.

'This is for the trophy, okay?' He threw the ball and I leapt, stretching out my hand. The ball hit my palm, stuck there, and I tumbled into the creek. Ben cheered, rushed over and lifted me out of the water.

'Lukey takes the catch!' he screamed. 'We win! The trophy is ours!'

He jumped and held me up, almost as if *I* was a trophy, then we both fell back laughing. Maggie joined in, singing from the jetty.

'Yeah, Maggie!' Ben yelled. 'We won!'

When we caught our breath, we sat in the water for a while. Dragonflies hovered about like miniature drones. A spangled drongo flew to meet its own shadow on a branch.

'You be right tomorrow?' Ben looked down at his creek-wrinkled hands. 'At school, I mean.' His voice was serious. He did that sometimes, like he'd taken over from Dad.

'Yeah,' I said, swallowing the lie. 'I'll be all right.'

He nodded. 'Good.'

As we headed for the house, Maggie swooped past us and waited on the verandah.

After Mum had said goodnight, I read about some more birds from the book. 'The wingspan of the royal albatross is three and a half metres.'

Ben stared at the ceiling. 'That's massive.'

I turned to another page. 'Crested bellbirds can throw their voices.'

'What does that mean?'

'It means, well, it sounds like it's right behind your shoulder, but it's really somewhere way in front of you.'

'Whoa. Weird.'

I shut the book and thought about what he'd asked me in the creek, about being okay at school.

'What about you?' I said. 'You okay about tomorrow?'

He didn't move. Just lay there with his hands behind his head,

crested bellbird

the lamplight falling on one side of his face. I never imagined he would be nervous, but maybe he was. 'I'll be fine, Lukey. Trust me.'

I put my book on the floor and switched off the lamp. The shapes of the room reappeared in the dark. The ceiling fan wobbled around and a flying fox screeched outside.

'Hey,' he whispered. 'Thanks for drawing the birds.'

'That's okay.'

'I reckon we'll win.'

'Yeah.'

'We can take the boat out every weekend, and every day in the holidays. Go fishing at The Pocket on a full moon. That's when the fish get really hungry.'

I kept the picture in my head: Ben and me in the boat, night birds calling from the trees, the stars reflected on the water like dots of paint.

The poinciana leaves shook near the window. Probably a possum. I forgot about boats and birds and thought about school the next day. That big maze of buildings had been empty all holidays and now we were about to fill it up again. I thought of all the kids scrambling past me through the gates, then how quickly they disappeared into classrooms, like hundreds of soldier crabs suddenly sinking into sand.

'Luke. You awake?'

I'd started to dream. Had to claw my way out of the sand and into the bedroom. 'Yeah?'

'You ever gonna open Dad's present?'

I yawned. 'Nope.'

'Gonna talk to him?'

'Dunno.'

'It's just a phone. Not that scary.'

I fell back into the sand with the crabs before he spoke again. 'And, Luke. What's that bird called again? The ugly one?'

'Um ... apostlebird?'

'That's it,' he said, rolling over in his bed. 'Ben and Luke, the apostlebirds.'

I was awake just enough to keep the joke going. 'Because we stick together?'

'Because we're ugly, loser.'

I couldn't see him in the dark, but I knew he was smiling.

CHAPTER 12

The Edge of the World

Ben and I wheeled our bikes out the gate. My backpack dug into my shoulders and the sun was stinging my eyes. My uniform was already faded and too big, handed down from Ben. He wore a collared shirt, untucked, and squinted at Mum as she took a photo. Then he rode small circles in front of our house, lifting the front wheel. I put my foot on the pedal, but Mum stepped in front of me and held the handlebars. Her face was in shadow. 'You sure you'll be okay?'

'Yep.'

'You remember which way to go?'

‘I’ve been riding to school for years, Mum.’

She tightened her grip. ‘But not without Ben.’

‘Yes I have.’

Ben stopped circling and laughed. ‘Yeah, and remember what happened?’

I remembered. I’d followed a bird down a laneway and into the bush. Chased it for ages, but never saw it properly. It could have been one of those vagrants Gem and I had talked about. By the time everyone found me, I’d missed half a day of school.

‘That was ages ago,’ I said. ‘I’ll be fine.’

She gave me a hug.

‘Bye, Mum.’

I pedalled down the drive and followed Ben as he wove along the road. Mum called out some last-minute instructions, waving goodbye, like we were sailing off to find the edge of the world.

Our street was long and flat and seemed to roll on forever, following the shape of the creek. After a few blocks, the houses became more crowded, until they were all boxed beside each other. The sun bounced off silver rooftops.

My shadow stretched across the road, pedalling in time. Ben rode ahead, angling across the bitumen, jumping gutters. It was already too hot for many birds to be out, but I heard a few calls from the neighbours' gardens. Miners and peewees, a gang of lorikeets shrieking at each other.

We cruised a few more blocks, then I heard a soft, scratchy song.

The vagrant.

I slowed down and stopped. It sang once more. I closed my eyes and thought of unzipping the bird book from my bag, but didn't dare make a sound. I turned my ear to the sky and waited for the call again.

'Come on, Luke!'

I looked up and Ben was way ahead of me, so I raced to catch up. We reached the corner and stopped on the footpath beside some shops.

'That bird again?' he said.

'Yeah.'

'Did you see it?'

'No. But I have to find it. I reckon it's a vagrant.'

'A what?'

magpie-lark (peewee)

'A vagrant. A bird that shouldn't be here. A bird that doesn't belong.'

We sat on our bikes. Old men walked in and out of the newsagency, clutching lotto tickets. A few mums and dads chatted outside a cafe, rocking prams, coffees in their hands.

'Hi!' A girl in a high school uniform stopped her bike beside us. It took me a second to recognise her because she was wearing a shiny black helmet instead of her floppy hat. 'You nervous?' Her eyes were on Ben.

He tapped a rhythm on his handlebars and shrugged. 'Not much. You?'

She made a scared face, with big eyes and clenched teeth. 'Sort of. I couldn't eat breakfast.'

'Yeah, me too, actually.' That was a lie. He'd wolfed his breakfast down like every other morning.

Handfuls of kids rode past us, down the road that led to the high school. Ben glanced at me. 'You'll be right, then?' He was using his Dad voice again.

I nodded, but I felt a bit like the lonely gull on the beach.

'Okay, meet you back here,' he said.

That was it. They went one way, I went the other. I rode slowly, looking at all the houses like they were photos in an album. I pedalled past the dog that had once hung around our yard for half a day, catching frisbees and ripping up our tennis balls. I passed the street where we'd once played cricket for an entire Saturday, kids flocking to the game like ants to a biscuit. And there was the patch of footpath where Ben punched a boy for calling me Bird Nerd. Right in the jaw, knocking him back into a wire fence. I remember Ben walked off like it was nothing. But it was definitely something.

A policewoman knocked on our door that night to talk with him and Mum at the dining table, while I sat on the back steps with Maggie. He said all the right things, that he was sorry and he'd never do it again. But later, with the lights off in our room, he said he'd always stick up for me. 'Trust me,' he said.

I reached the school gate and parked my bike in the racks. Kids streamed past me. The uniform stuck to my skin as I slipped off the backpack. I breathed hard and looked back down the street, counting the blocks all the way to the shops. Someone was there, sitting on a bike.

Ben.

He'd watched me all the way. It was too far for our eyes to meet, but the moment I saw him, he spun his bike around and rode off towards the high school.

CHAPTER 13

Crested Pigeon

We weren't the only ones who wanted a boat. It was all anyone talked about for that first day back. Even kids who already had boats were going to enter and everyone had worked out a different way to win.

A girl called Sophie was writing a play about the creek, which her family would perform for the judges. 'Just working out costumes at the moment and rehearsals begin next week,' she announced at the bag racks.

Bertie, who was good with words, had been interviewing older locals, collecting stories about the creek into a sort of newspaper. 'It's called *The Cabbage Tree Chronicle*,' he said, unrolling a draft of the front page as we walked into the classroom.

Just before the first lesson started, the whole room fell silent as Willow unveiled a series of small painted scenes of the creek. The boat ramp, a sunset reflected in the water, and a purple cloud rolling above the tree line. 'These are just my practice pictures,' she said.

We all gulped at the thought of her finished paintings.

I didn't tell anyone about our book. I knew most of the kids in my class, but no-one was into birds. And without Ben in the school, not many people noticed me. I faded, like my uniform. So I didn't say much. Sat at a desk by the window and watched a crow perch on the monkey bars. It knew that a meal of sandwich crusts and chip crumbs was just a few hours away.

Our teacher, Mr Knight, was new to the school. He was a short man with a bushy moustache darker than his wispy blond hair, and his voice bounced up and down like a handball. He talked about rules and routines, pacing between all the desks, as if he wanted to hear himself speak from every spot in the room. Then he said something about 'useless things' and even his pinball voice couldn't keep me interested. I stared out the window again. A pair of crested pigeons had replaced the crow in the playground. I'd already drawn one for *The Birds of Cabbage Tree Creek*, but I wondered if I'd made it colourful enough. Looking at them now, the feathers on their wings gleamed like tiny gemstones.

'I'm sorry I can't hold your attention like those birds, young man.'

I turned around. Mr Knight stood a few desks away. Along with everyone else, he was staring at me. I couldn't read his face, but his moustache twitched.

'Um, sorry,' I said.

'You know what to do?' His voice wasn't bouncy now. Flat as the creek on a still day.

The other kids had pencils poised over sheets of paper.

'Yes.'

He nodded and continued his journey around the room.

Jade sat at the desk next to

crested pigeon

mine. A stack of scented erasers stood like a colourful castle beside her pencil case. I could smell bubblegum and lemonade.

'What do we have to do?' I whispered.

She didn't look up. 'Write your name at the top, then draw something useless and important.'

'But ... how can something be useless *and* important?'

She twirled a pencil between her fingers. 'Useless to everyone else,' she said, 'but important to you.'

'Oh. Okay.'

I had no idea. Couldn't think of anything. I looked back outside and the crested pigeons were gone.

CHAPTER 14

Ordinary

After school, Ben and I met at the shops. We rode home with the sun on our backpacks.

'What was it like?' I said, pushing the pedals hard to keep up.

'All right. Kinda boring. Got lost a few times.'

'The ovals big?'

'Yeah, huge.'

'What are the teachers like?'

'They're like teachers.'

'Did you know anyone?'

'Yeah, a few.'

'What did you do at lunch?'

'What did *you* do – think of a hundred questions to ask me?'

He stood tall on his pedals, then made his bike hop along the road. I took my right hand off the handlebars, then my left, rode no hands for a few seconds, but the front wheel wobbled so I grabbed on again.

'I got a new teacher,' I said. 'Mr Knight.'

'What's he like?'

'A teacher.' I grinned.

We rode on and the houses grew further apart as we got closer to home. Ben caught my eye. 'Race ya?'

I didn't answer. Just took off. Pedalled hard, straight for our place. He chased me, came up beside my bike, hammering his feet in blurry circles. I pedalled faster, edging my wheel in front of his. Then he laughed and raced ahead.

When he reached our house, he charged up the driveway and kept riding, right past the house and off to the creek. 'Watch this, Lukey!' He steered his speeding bike onto the jetty, bumped along the planks and flew straight into the water.

I couldn't believe it. He'd gone under, bike and all.

He came back up, choked with laughter, raising his hands as if accepting the applause of a whole stadium. I rode to the edge of the creek and he dragged his bike to the bank.

I pointed to the dripping school bag still strapped to his back. 'Hope you don't have any homework.'

Later, on the verandah, I told him about everything the kids in my class were doing to win the boat. It was the same at his high school. He'd heard stories of sculptures, songs and short stories. Someone was making a music video, and there was talk of a town mural. A book of bird drawings suddenly seemed a bit ordinary.

'Is there anything else we can do?' I said, picking at a bowl of chips.

'I can do heaps of stuff, but you're hopeless,' he said, grinning as he pegged a chip at my head.

'Hopeless?' I threw one back at him. 'Who's drawing all the pictures?'

He didn't say anything. Just threw another chip and I tried to catch it in my mouth.

'Maybe we need more birds,' I said. 'And I gotta find the one I don't know. Imagine if I found an exotic parrot around here that no-one even knew about. A vagrant.'

He nodded. 'Let's just keep going. It's still a good idea, I reckon.' He edged some brightness into his voice, but he was hardly dancing around the backyard.

We spent the afternoon at the creek, trying to add to our list, but only spied a couple of new birds: a darter drying its wings on a branch and a rainbow bee-eater that dived for bugs not far from the white boat. I messed up a few of my drawings. Ben lazed against trees instead of climbing them. Neither of us said so, but it was getting harder to picture ourselves discovering hidden islands, fishing at The Pocket or even paddling to the other side.

darter

CHAPTER 15

An Unfinished Bird

About a week later, I stopped at the shops after school, but Ben didn't turn up. I waited for a while, thinking every kid in a white collared shirt could be him, until there were none left. I rode home, slowly at first, wondering where he was. Then the wonder turned to worry and I rode faster. The hot wind hit me like a hairdryer and my eyes blurred with tears. I sped up the drive, propped my bike against the house and something smacked me in the face. It burst and drenched my uniform. I wiped the water from my eyes, looked up and froze. There was a girl half-hiding behind the poinciana, with an armful of water balloons, her face turned pale with shock.

'Sorry,' she said. 'Thought you were Ben.'

At that moment, another balloon whacked me in the back of the head and soaked my school bag. I shook the water from my hair, turned around and glared at Ben, who stood with his own pile of balloons.

'Oh, I thought you were Frankie,' he said.

I spun back around as Frankie stepped out from behind the tree. I scowled for a second, then I left them with their loaded balloons and walked up the steps, dripping a trail of water all the way to our room. I scrubbed my hair with a towel and changed clothes. Then I sat at the verandah table, ate a chocolate biscuit and flicked through my sketchbook. Maggie arrived to peck at crumbs under my chair.

'Did you know she was here?' I frowned at Maggie. 'Did you see her behind the tree?'

If she knew, she was keeping it to herself. I turned to a new page and started the soft, scribbly outline of a royal spoonbill. Ben and Frankie came up the

stairs. She looked different without a floppy hat or helmet on. Her hair was short and messy.

'You know Luke,' Ben said to her. 'Oh, and this is Maggie.'

Frankie smiled as Maggie bounced onto the table and gargled a welcome. Then she turned her eyes to my sketchbook. 'What are you drawing?'

The answer appeared in my head, but it didn't come out. My pencil shook.

'Luke draws birds,' said Ben. I waited for more, but that was all he said. He didn't tell her about *The Birds of Cabbage Tree Creek*. He didn't say we wanted to win a boat. He didn't mention the buckets of fish or sleeping under the stars, or that the whole thing was his idea.

'Cute,' she said.

Cute. Like I was five years old. I closed the book, walked inside and fell on my bed. I didn't finish the spoonbill. Left it floating on the page without any legs. I felt a bit the same, like an anchor had come loose and I'd started to drift away.

CHAPTER 16

Thick Smoke

'Dad wants to see you.' Mum's words hit me like a footy in the guts. She was perched on a kitchen stool with a cup of peppermint tea. I'd just filled the sink with hot water and soapy bubbles. Ben twirled a tea towel, waiting to dry up.

'*See* me – why?'

'He's your father.'

'But—'

'Listen, love. I know this is hard. But he's in town soon, staying at Gran's for a while. I think it's time to take some steps forward. You can't stay angry forever.' She'd been reading that website again.

'He ran away. Why can't I be mad?'

She studied her tea, as if it could tell her what to say next. 'He just wants to see you again.'

I clanged the cutlery into the sink. 'When?'

'This weekend.' She took a sip. 'He's going to pick you up and you can go wherever you like. Show him some birds, if you want.'

'What about Ben? Is he getting kidnapped too?'

'Luke!' The word shot out of her mouth. She was serious now. 'Ben's doing fine with your dad. This is about you.'

Ben patted my head like I was a little dog. 'You can do it, big guy.'

Mum clinked her cup down on the bench, like a full stop to finish the conversation. She turned to Ben. 'Frankie seems nice.'

'Is she your girlfriend, big guy?' I hadn't been able to form any words this afternoon. Now they slipped out when I should have swallowed them.

'She's not my *girl*friend.' He flicked me with the towel.

Mum ignored us. 'Is she in your class?'

'Yep.' He twisted the scrunched-up tea towel

inside a wet glass, squeaking it dry. 'She just moved here.'

I dunked some bowls into the hot water and scrubbed them with a brush.

'And how's the book going?' She looked back at me. Everyone was forgetting that this was *our* book, not just mine.

'Still haven't found that bird.'

'Ooh, a mystery,' she said.

'Everyone else is doing better stuff. And we're not gonna find many more birds.'

'Why not?'

I stopped scrubbing and looked out the kitchen window. I could see the creek but only as much as the window frame allowed, a tiny rectangular piece of the whole puzzle. That was the problem. How could I draw all the birds of Cabbage Tree Creek when I couldn't get to see most of it?

'They're not around here,' I said. 'The other birds, I mean. They live in other parts of the creek.'

I stacked the dripping bowls on the rack. Ben grabbed one and towelled it dry.

'I've got it!' He widened his eyes and pointed

a finger in the air. 'You wanna find more birds, right?'

'Yeah.'

'So we can win the boat?'

'Yeah.'

'Then there's one thing we need. One thing that'll help you see all the birds.'

'What?'

He edged his excited face closer to mine. 'A boat!'

I shoved him and he fell over laughing. It was just a joke, a stupid throwaway line. Words that should have wisped away. But they hung in the kitchen like thick smoke until my eyes watered and a lump scratched in my throat. Mum tried to fold me up in a hug, but I ran outside and down the steps. Wiped away my tears and breathed in the cool air. Currawongs chattered themselves to rest. A koel sang a falling note from a neighbour's tree. A pair of turtle-doves cooed each other goodnight. All birds I'd already drawn.

CHAPTER 17

Emerald Dove

The next day after school, Ben and I tramped along the track to the old windmill. Everything from the night before was still churning in my head, and we hadn't talked much all day. I only followed him because sometimes there were birds nesting in the windmill, but I didn't know he'd invited Frankie too.

'Hey, dudes.' She sat in a tree along the path, waiting for us. Her floppy hat shaded half of her face and she picked out the last few crumbs from a chip packet. Then she pushed herself off the branch, landed with a thud and saluted like an Olympic gymnast. Ben clapped and I rolled my eyes.

When we reached the windmill, I focused my binoculars on a dove scratching around on the opposite bank.

'Can I have a look?' Frankie held out her hand. I scanned her face to work out if she was teasing me, then I passed the binoculars to her.

'I see it,' she said. 'What's it called?'

'Emerald dove.'

'Cool.' She asked more questions and I told her whatever I knew about emerald doves.

'You sound like my dad,' she said. 'He's into birds.'

'Really?'

She spun the binoculars around the wrong way and pointed them at me. 'Wow, you look tiny!' She let out a bouncy laugh and gave the binoculars back to me.

'Where did you live before?' I said.

'With Mum, not that far from here. I just moved in with Dad coz it's closer to the high school.'

'Do you still see your mum?'

'Yeah. All the time.'

emerald dove

I wondered how long her parents had lived apart. Maybe forever. She talked so easily about it.

'Hey, Frankie!' Ben waved from halfway up the windmill. 'You coming?'

Her face broke into a wide grin. She climbed up the metal frame, grabbing the rungs and scrambling up the poles like she did it every day. When she was next to Ben, she looked down. 'You wanna come up?'

Ben knew it was way too high for me and I shook my head. She shrugged like it didn't matter and they both climbed to the top. I couldn't have kicked a footy that high if I tried. They were so far up I couldn't hear what they were saying, only Frankie's laugh as it flew down from the windmill and skipped around the creek.

CHAPTER 18

A Ball of Dirt

Later in the week, I rode behind Ben and Frankie on the way home from school. It had rained at lunchtime so the road was still wet and clouds of steam rose from the bitumen. Ben was trying to ride as far as he could on one wheel and Frankie rode no hands. She sat tall with her arms crossed as if it was the easiest thing in the world.

I got sick of watching them show off, so I pedalled faster to get around them. My tyres flicked thin sprays of water into the air. As I rode closer, I heard them talking. Ben wanted to take something, but I didn't know what. That was all I heard because they stopped talking as I went past.

A block further on I heard the call again. The soft, scratchy sound that had bugged me for weeks. I squeezed the brakes, skidded to a stop and laid my bike on the footpath. I remembered Gem's advice. Stood still. Waited. The mystery bird squeaked again, not from a tree but somewhere among the houses, behind the fences. A ground parrot? It didn't sound like one.

The whirring hum of bike tyres came up behind me.

'Watcha doing?' Frankie said. Ben sat on his bike next to her.

I kept an eye on the houses. 'There's a bird.'

'Where?'

'Don't know. Somewhere.'

'How do you know?'

'I can hear it.'

Frankie held her chin high and squinted. 'Oh yeah, I hear it. It's called a crow. Very rare.' Her mouth was still, but there was a spark in her eyes. 'Why do you care so much?'

'What do you mean?'

She snorted. 'It's just a bird.'

My jaw tightened. The air around me suddenly felt warm and thick. *Just a bird.* It was like saying the moon was just a rock or Earth was just a ball of dirt. She hadn't been like this with the emerald dove the other day.

'Maybe she's right, Luke.'

I threw Ben a death-stare. 'What?'

'Why do you have to find *that* bird so badly?'

'Because ... because it's a vagrant.'

'So?'

My eyes itched and my head throbbed. He didn't understand. I wasn't even sure if I did. There was something about this bird, lost and out of place. I knew what that was like. Gem did too. But maybe Ben never felt lost. He was always exactly where he should be, like he was here first and the rest of the world grew around him.

All that sounded stupid in my head, so I kept it simple. 'I just want to win the boat.'

Frankie planted her feet back on the pedals. 'That one little bird isn't gonna win it,' she said. 'Forget about it, Bird Nerd.'

She rode away and I looked at Ben. His

mouth twitched, but he didn't say a word. I couldn't believe it. My face felt hot and my whole body burned with hurt. He could have at least said something. Stuck up for me.

CHAPTER 19

Even the Small Ones

The back wall of our classroom had started to fill up with drawings of the useless and important things in all our lives.

Emma had drawn an earring shaped like a musical note. 'It's a semi-quaver. My grandma gave me a pair, but I lost one. So now I can't wear it.'

Mr Knight looked at the ceiling like he was trying to solve a tricky maths problem. 'Have you thought about wearing earrings that don't match?'

She looked at him like he'd asked her to gut a fish.

Deshan pinned up a picture of a fishing rod. 'It's too small and the reel doesn't work anymore, but I caught my first fish with it at The Pocket.'

'How big was the fish?' Mr Knight's moustache curled a bit.

'This big,' said Deshan, measuring the memory of the fish with his hands. The class erupted into whines of disbelief.

Other kids had sketched snow globes, animal statues or clothes they'd worn as babies. I still didn't know what to draw. Whenever I thought of something important – bike, binoculars or bird guide – I couldn't imagine how it could ever be useless.

After school, I sat in the back of the ute with Gem. We were stopped beside an open park. A line of ibises marched slowly across the grass, poking curved beaks into the ground. We picked sugary peanuts from a bag as Gem tried to guess my mystery bird.

Australian white ibis

'Scaly-breasted lorikeet. Little lorikeet. Musk lorikeet. Ever heard a musk lorikeet, Lukey Luke?'

I shook my head. 'I've seen them before. Whatever it is, it's not from around here.'

'Oh, then maybe it's a monkey.'

'What?'

'An elephant?'

'Hilarious.'

'Or a polar bear. They're not from around here. And they squeak like parrots when they're angry.' Her eyes widened as she tried to look serious. But then she cracked into her cockatoo laugh and pushed my arm.

'You finished now?' I laughed.

'Yeah, sorry,' she said. 'You're probably right – a bird from somewhere else.'

'A vagrant,' I said, enjoying the sound of the word.

We watched the ibises stride across the park. They looked like a search party, studying every patch of grass, with wings folded like arms by their sides.

'It's good you're seeing your dad on the weekend.'

I said nothing.

'You looking forward to it?'

I kept quiet so the conversation would wither away, like a fire without any fuel.

'Fine. How long till you have to hand in your book?'

'A few weeks,' I said, digging the last few peanuts out of the bag. 'But I'm not sure if I will. Even if I do find that bird.'

'Why not?'

'Don't think Ben wants to do it anymore.'

Gem straightened up and poked me in the arm. 'Listen, Mr Brown Thornbill. You might think Ben's a big wedge-tailed eagle, but he's not the boss. You remember how long birds have been around?'

It was one of the first facts Gem had taught me. 'Over sixty million years.'

'That's right! Thousands of different birds, flapping around for that long, doing what they need to do to survive. And they're all as important as each other, even the small ones.' Her eyes weren't blinking. 'Get what I'm trying to say?'

I scratched my arm and shrugged. 'Um, sort of.'

'You gotta fly your own path, little bird. Do what *you* want to do.'

CHAPTER 20

Gone

I woke one morning to the sound of blue-faced honeyeaters squawking outside our window. They looked like feathered superheroes, with sleek blue masks and wings for capes. I sat up and threw a rolled pair of socks at Ben.

'Time to get up.' I yawned.

The bed was empty.

'Ben?'

The lounge room was empty too. Even my present from Dad wasn't there anymore. Mum must have put it away.

blue-faced honeyeater

'Ben!'

He wasn't digging into a cereal box in the kitchen. Not on the verandah. His bag was missing from its usual spot by the door.

Mum walked out of the steamy bathroom, pulling a brush through her hair.

'Where's Ben?' I said.

'Oh, he's gone.'

I followed her into her room. 'Where?'

She rummaged through a box of chunky rings beside her bed. 'There's a note on the fridge.'

I raced back to the kitchen. The note was scribbled on the back of an envelope.

Early footy training at school – Ben.

He hadn't told me much about high school, but I knew one thing: footy didn't start for another few months. He was up to something.

CHAPTER 21

Just a Tree

The weekend came and I had Gem's voice in my head, telling me to do what I wanted. I grabbed my sketchbook and bounded down the steps. There were birds to find.

Maggie swooped from tree to tree as I ran beside the creek, but we stopped at the old white boat. It still hadn't moved.

'Maybe Ben's right,' I said to Maggie. 'They wouldn't notice if it was gone.'

She squawked at me.

'Don't worry. I'm not gonna steal it. We'll have our own boat soon enough. Even if Ben doesn't help.'

She shook her feathers and darted off in a different direction.

'See ya, then.'

I ran on, pushed through a curtain of leaves and came to the Jumping Tree. I sat on the dirt, held my binoculars and waited.

Pick a spot. The birds will come. That was what Gem always said.

But it didn't work. The tide rose over my feet and all I saw was a handful of birds I'd already put in the book. Ducks, swallows and the same white-faced heron that always stalked around here.

Then I heard voices. I knew straightaway it was Ben and Frankie, getting closer.

'It's a pretty old boat,' Frankie said. 'Do you know who owns it?'

'Nah,' said Ben. 'But who cares.'

'When are you gonna take it?'

'Middle of the night, I reckon. When everyone's asleep.'

Were they talking about the white boat? I'd never thought Ben was serious about taking it.

They stepped into the clearing.

white-faced heron

'Luke! What are you doing here?'

He took off his cap and his hair stuck to his forehead. Frankie squirted water from a drink bottle onto her face.

'Drawing birds,' I said, looking back at the creek. 'Gotta win a boat, remember?'

I waited for him to say it was hopeless, for her to call me Bird Nerd. But they didn't. Instead, they sat next to me on the muddy bank. I tipped my head back. A brahminy kite sailed across the sky. I listened, straining to hear above the blowflies and cicadas. Then a soft, rattly squeak cut through the air – the bird I was chasing. I closed my eyes and pictured a colourful bird with a long tail. I knew it from my bird guide, but it didn't make sense. The bird in my head was a desert bird, a world away from Cabbage Tree Creek. Not even vagrants got *that* lost.

'You still looking for that bird?' Frankie said.

I opened my eyes. 'Did you hear it?'

Her face was blank, an empty page. 'You're not gonna find it.'

'How do you know?'

She shrugged and faced the water. 'Do you really think a book of birds will win?'

I turned to Ben. He looked down, digging lines into the mud with a stick. 'I don't know anymore, Luke.'

'What's wrong with you?' My voice grew louder. 'Don't you want a boat? Don't you want to go to The Pocket?'

'Everyone else is doing such cool stuff, Lukey. And you said you won't find many more birds, right?'

I knew it. He thought *The Birds of Cabbage Tree Creek* was stupid. After all the pictures I'd drawn, he thought the whole thing was a waste of time. And while I'd been looking for more birds, he'd already given up and was hanging out with Frankie instead.

'Ben's got another plan.' Frankie grinned.

I glared at her, then at him. 'What is it?'

He shook his head. 'Nothing.'

'It must be better than a book of birds. Tell me.'

'I can't.'

'Why not?'

'I just can't!'

His eyes told me to shut up. Then I remembered what I'd heard them talking about. Stealing the boat in the middle of the night. That was why he couldn't tell me.

Frankie stood up and stretched her arms above her head. 'It's jumpin' time, I reckon.'

They climbed the tree and sprang off the branch, falling through the sky, crashing into the creek. They jumped together a few times, holding hands. The splashes grew louder. I dug my fingernails into my palms and a knot of anger twisted in my gut.

After another jump, Frankie shot back up through the water. She shook her hair and droplets flicked around like a sprinkler. 'Hope we're not scaring the birds away,' she said. 'Is that why you don't jump? Because it'll scare them?'

Ben laughed. 'Can't really call it the Jumping Tree if you don't jump, Lukey. It's just a tree, then.'

It was nothing, really. Another joke, but enough to push me onto my feet. 'Then I'll jump.'

I dropped the sketchbook and pencil, then slipped off my shirt and threw it on the ground.

The paperbark was soft as I dug my fingers into the trunk and lifted myself up, scrambled to the heavy branch that rose up and out over the water. Holding tight, I edged along. Tried to fix my eyes on something still – a dead tree across the creek – but the branch started to wobble and shake. My hands trembled. Leaves danced and the tree groaned, like it wanted to shake me off. Everything rocked backwards and forwards like I was swaying on a playground swing. I shut my eyes and didn't move.

I clung to the branch for an hour. Or a few seconds. I couldn't tell. Something nudged me from behind and I opened my eyes.

'Lukey,' whispered Ben. 'It's all right.' He put his hand on my back. I breathed deep. 'You don't have to, Luke. Just come back down.'

I looked at the water below, a deep coffee-coloured pool waiting to swallow me up. I wanted to jump but I couldn't. I crawled back along the branch and followed Ben down the trunk. Then I grabbed my stuff and ran into the bush.

'Luke, wait!'

I didn't. My feet pounded the dirt track.

Branches tore at my arms. My chest burned. Finally, I stopped halfway along the path, surrounded by tangled scrub. Caught my breath and smudged tears across my face with the back of my hand. I held *The Birds of Cabbage Tree Creek* and flipped through the pages, all the pictures I'd drawn. I thought about the stories Ben and I had dreamt up. Catching buckets of fish, sleeping under the stars – just us and the birds.

But it wasn't just us anymore. And Ben and Frankie were right. A book of birds would never win. I chucked it into the bush and ran home.

CHAPTER 22

A Shark in the Sky

That afternoon, I sat on the grass outside our house and waited for Dad. I had my birding gear in a backpack beside me. Ants crawled over my sneakers and a fly buzzed round my head. Mum sat on the front steps and asked if I was okay, again and again. I didn't know where Ben was. Probably up a tree, sharing secrets with Frankie.

The fly droned a dizzy circle and landed on my face. A sword of sunlight hit me in the eye. Then a car revved into our street and my throat stung. I didn't want to do this. Didn't want to talk to him and pretend everything was normal, didn't want to shake his hand like Ben had told me to. My breath shook and I rubbed my eyes. Mum asked again if I was okay, but I didn't answer. I jumped to my feet, grabbed the backpack and ran.

My shoes smacked the bitumen as I charged down the road. Mum yelled something, but all I heard was my breath, gasping louder and louder. My head felt like a waterlogged footy, and the trees and houses were fuzzy blobs. I bolted down the street, turned a corner and ran on. Didn't know where I was going, but I kept running, further away from home, from Dad and his stupid handshake. I sprinted a few more blocks, flipped over a fence and staggered across a park that hadn't been mown in a hundred years. I collapsed in the long grass and scrunched my eyes. Waited for the drumroll in my chest to slow down and hoped no-one would find me.

Distant noises wavered in the air. Cars hummed. Trains squeaked in and out of a station. A bit closer, fairy-wrens chattered in the thick grass. I wished Maggie was around, but I hadn't seen her since the morning. I lay half-asleep as the afternoon stretched out like a thin cloud.

'Get up, idiot.'

I opened my eyes. Ben's face was framed by the hazy grey sky.

'How did you find me?'

'Just get up!' He kicked my foot. 'Mum's freaking out.'

He turned and pushed his way through the grass. I swung the backpack onto my shoulder and jogged to catch up. 'How long have I been gone?'

'Ages. Mum and Gem had a big fight on the phone.'

'Why?'

He stopped on the footpath and pierced me with his dark eyes. 'Because you ran off and Mum blamed Gem. Said she's always hiding you from Dad.'

'But—'

'Just shut up and keep walking.'

I followed his orders and scuffed along the streets that twisted like eels, back to our road. He marched in front and I shuffled in his shadow, like a dog on an invisible lead.

'Are Mum and Gem still looking for me?'

'Probably.' He kept his head down.

'What about Dad?'

He stormed along the footpath. A dark cloud drifted above us, like a giant shark in the sky. 'He went back to Gran's.'

I slowed down. Tried to picture Mum and Gem fighting, and Dad slamming the car door before driving away.

'You're making everything worse.' Ben spat the words over his shoulder. 'Why don't you just grow up?'

A blast of thunder shook the suburb. The clouds swelled and turned the sky a murky black, like a swirling ocean at night. We ran the rest of the way and when Mum saw us coming, she rushed at me. I thought she was going to knock me over, but she squeezed me in a hug until I nearly choked. She was still mad and kept yelling at me, but she wouldn't let go. Then the ocean in the sky started to fall, sheets of rain drenching our clothes.

We ran up the back steps and watched the

storm from the verandah. Rain sloshed up the creek and trees thrashed in the wind.

'Sorry, Mum.'

She draped a towel over my wet shoulders. 'You just weren't ready.'

'Is Gem mad?'

'She'll be fine.'

'Does Dad hate me?'

She shook her head. 'Of course not. He's your father.'

I had a feeling she wouldn't bother me about seeing him for a while, but Ben's words hammered in my head like the rain on the roof. Maybe I had to grow up.

CHAPTER 23

Full of Holes

Everyone else had drawn their useless and important things. The back wall of the classroom was covered with pictures of broken toys, stuffed animals and old books. I should have been thinking of my own thing, but instead I stared out the window. A yellow robin fluttered into the garden. It seemed to pose for me, clinging to a thin stem, but I didn't even reach for my pencil. I hadn't drawn a single bird since I'd thrown the book away.

Mr Knight came in and strode around the desks. His voice bounced like a ping-pong ball as

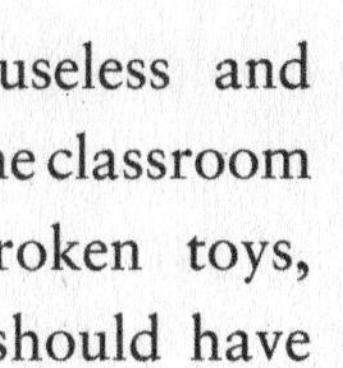

eastern yellow robin

he recited the plan for the day. Then he talked about the pictures on the back wall.

'Everyone has done a wonderful job,' he said. 'Well, almost everyone.' He shot me a look, but his moustache curved into a smile. It was like his eyes and moustache were saying different things at the same time. 'Does anybody remember why I asked you to draw these things?'

I didn't. Luckily, Jade raised her hand. 'Because it shows who we are.'

'That's right,' he said. 'By revealing something that is important to you – and only you – we find out what you value and the sort of person you are.'

I hadn't drawn anything. What did that say about me?

'So I thought I should draw a picture too. An important and useless thing of my own.' He held a drawing up to the class. My heart beat faster when I saw it. I leant forward. For the first time all year, I wanted to hear what Mr Knight had to say. 'This is the boat I had when I was your age. My brother and I were in it almost every day. Best time of our lives.'

'Did you go fishing?' said Deshan.

'We did. Never caught anything as big as the fish you caught, though, Deshan.' There was a hint of a grin again.

Emma put up her hand. 'But why is it useless?'

'It's old and full of cracks. You can't see them, but if I took that boat onto Cabbage Tree Creek today, it'd sink to the bottom before it even got wet.'

I wondered how many more weird jokes were hiding in that moustache. But there was something bigger I had to ask. 'What colour was it?' I said.

Mr Knight looked straight at me. 'White.'

I clenched my hands under the desk. 'And where is it now?'

His eyes and moustache worked together this time, completely still. 'Well, it's too special to throw away. So it's tied to a fence post in my backyard. If you've ever walked along that part of the creek, you might have seen it.'

I swallowed hard and all at once I felt hot, the sun angling through the glass onto my desk. Mr Knight still faced me, but spoke to the whole class as he asked us to get our spelling books ready. Then he walked to the back of the room and pinned his drawing to the wall.

CHAPTER 24

Ben's Side of the Room

I rode home as fast as a falcon. The whole suburb was a blur. All I could think about was the cracks in Mr Knight's boat and Ben's plan to steal it in the middle of the night. I raced up the stairs and into our room. Ben's side was a mess. The floor was layered with dirty socks, wet towels and muesli bar wrappers. It reminded me of a garden bed we'd made at school last year, built up with layers of newspaper and compost. I had a feeling something might sprout from the dark corners of this room too.

I didn't really know what I was looking for. Plans to steal the boat, maybe – a map or a list of steps? I pushed aside a pile of schoolbooks on his desk and an apple core rolled onto the floor. More compost. There was a scatter of pencil shavings, a collection of stones from the creek and a taped-up tennis ball we used for cricket. Then I saw a picture, drawn on a scrap from an exercise book. It was a bird, hunched on a branch. I recognised it straightaway – an apostlebird. It was a pretty good drawing.

'What are you doing?' Ben ripped the picture from my hand. He scrunched it up and threw it under his bed.

'Did you draw that?' I said.

'None of your business.' His dark eyes glared from under the cliffs of his eyebrows.

I stepped over junk to get to my side of the room. 'Why are you drawing birds if you think the book's so stupid?'

'I never said that.'

'You gave up on it. And I know what you're gonna do. I'm telling Mum.'

'Telling her what?'

I took a deep breath. This was it. 'That you're gonna steal the boat.'

His mouth fell open and he narrowed his eyes. 'What? Whose boat?'

'The old white boat – my teacher's boat. I heard you and Frankie talking. You're gonna take it in the middle of the night.'

His face reddened. He shook his head. 'You think I'd steal a boat? You really think I'd do that?'

I took a step back. 'I heard you talking.'

'You heard wrong,' he said through clenched teeth.

I was in the doorway now. 'Then what were you talking about?'

He sat on his bed and looked down, twisting his fingers in his hands. 'I can't say. You'll get mad. You just gotta trust me.'

'Still sounds like you're gonna steal the—'

'How could you think that?' he yelled. There were tears in his eyes.

All my life, I knew I could bug my brother. I'd done it every day. But until now, I had no idea I could upset him.

'Tell me,' I said.

He locked his fingers together and looked around the room, at the footy posters, the broken fishing reel, the empty biscuit box on the floor. Then he faced me again. 'Just get out.'

'But—'

'Get out!'

He stood up and slammed the door. I stumbled and fell back onto the floorboards. I lay there, looking up at the ceiling, with one thought pounding in my head.

My brother hated me.

CHAPTER 25

Moving Out

The next day was Saturday. The chill of early autumn seeped into the house like a slow-moving tide. I sat on the edge of my bed, the floorboards cold under my feet.

He took the small things first. Shoes, football, bits and pieces off his desk. Then he tipped his clothes into a laundry basket and carried them out. He wheeled his desk chair away, then dragged the desk. Mum helped him tilt the bed on its side to get it through the doorway. They covered the wardrobe with blankets and walked it along the floor, bearing its weight like it was an old man limping in from the cold.

That was it. Ben had moved out of our room and into Mum's study. But it wasn't called the study anymore. It was Ben's Room.

Mum appeared at my door. She walked silently in her socks, sat on the bed and I closed my eyes as she held me tight.

CHAPTER 26

The Only Thing Left

First Dad, now Ben. Powerful owls, both of them. I wandered to the backyard and found Maggie on a low white branch, facing the creek. Hadn't seen her since the day before.

'Where've you been?'

She turned to my voice, then back to the water. I sat against the tree and stabbed the ground with a stick. I thought of Ben slamming the door. He'd asked me to trust him. Told me to grow up. And I hadn't. No wonder he'd moved out of our room.

'I've wrecked everything, Maggie. Ben hates me. The book's gone. We're never gonna win the boat. Maybe he's right – I just make everything worse.'

She was still, her beak raised, like she was deep in thought. I sometimes wondered if she was more than a bird and if there was a bigger reason I'd found her on the road that day. Not magic and not Dad in disguise or anything. I just liked to imagine I was *supposed* to find her, like it was meant to happen. Now she was about the only thing I had left.

She gargled to the sky and blinked her chocolate-brown eyes. I said thanks, left her on the branch and shuffled back to the house.

A few days later, she was gone too.

CHAPTER 27

A Dried-up Creek

I wasn't worried at first. She sometimes disappeared for a whole day, gliding back to the yard in the late afternoon. But when she'd been missing for three days, I knew something wasn't right. I stood on the verandah and felt the emptiness in the air. A dog barked. A lawnmower chugged. But the poinciana stood still, not a single bird in its branches.

Mum let me stay home and I trekked along the bank of the creek all day. Past the boat, the Jumping Tree, further than I'd ever been. I called Maggie's name and scanned the tallest gum trees until my neck was sore. The sun threw its last splash of light on the leaves and I tripped over tree roots on my way home in the dark. Walked slowly across the cold grass, up the back steps and straight through the dining room. Ben and Mum were shapes at the table.

'Lukey, you okay?'

'Luke, love. Dinner's ready.'

I stopped and turned around. Ben's dark eyes. Mum's half-smile.

'Thanks,' I said. 'But I'm not hungry.'

The rest of the week dragged. I watched and waited, wandered the creek. But she didn't come. For nearly a year, I had woken to the same song, the same friend swooping from the poinciana down to the verandah railing, dressed in that black-and-white feathery suit.

My days were empty, like a dried-up creek.

And at night, I fell onto my bed and wished for the mattress to swallow me whole.

CHAPTER 28

Tawny Frogmouths

By Friday, I couldn't stand it. Maggie was gone. Ben was never home. The house was too quiet, like every room was holding its breath. I had to get away. Had to get out of my half-empty room, a big blank reminder of when Ben and I had been proper brothers, a pair of ugly apostlebirds. So I grabbed the tent from under the house and carried it to the end of the yard.

I unfolded it and dragged each corner across the grass. It didn't stretch into a square the way it was supposed to and I couldn't tell the front from the back. I stabbed pegs into the corners but they stopped halfway, couldn't even whack them in further with the mallet. Tried pushing the poles through the slots. They got stuck. I ripped out the pegs, bundled everything into a messy pile and threw it under the house.

On the verandah, Mum and Gem fished for Scrabble tiles in a cloth bag. A bowl of pretzels sat on the table and a glass water bottle overlooked the board between them, like a referee.

'Tent ready?' Gem lined up her tiles.

I slumped on the daybed against the wall. 'Nope.'

'Want some help?' said Mum.

'No. Thanks.'

Mum and Gem started their game, intersecting words across the board. A salty breeze swam by, like the creek's final sigh before dark.

'It won't last forever, Luke.' Mum rearranged her letters.

'What?'

'Maggie'll come back.'

'How do you know?'

She shrugged. She didn't really know.

'And this thing with Ben,' she said. 'It'll get better. You'll always be brothers.'

I got up and poured water from the bottle into a glass. A slice of lime tumbled in as well. 'Doesn't feel like we're brothers. Not like it used to.'

Gem placed a word on the board.

'No way!' cried Mum.

'What?' Gem added up the points.

'*Za* is not a word.'

'It means pizza.'

'Rubbish. It's just a couple of letters from *pizza*.'

Gem wrote down the score. Mum poked out her tongue and threw a pretzel at her sister. They both laughed.

'I remember when your mum started high school,' Gem said to me. 'Dropped me like a sack of potatoes.'

Mum nodded, eyes on the game. 'I was horrible.'

'Awful.'

'Hideous.'

Mum placed another word on the board.

tawny frogmouth

'You know what it reminds me of?' Gem looked at me and forgot the game for a moment. 'Tawny frogmouths. Remember the tawnies last year?'

I sipped my water and squinted at the memory. A pair of tawny frogmouths had made a home in Gem's brush box last spring. It was a scrappy nest, just a handful of sticks wedged into a fork of the tree. We watched them take turns on the eggs for weeks, then one day, we spotted two chicks peeking out from the nest. Little balls of fluff, the colour of campfire ash. Eyes like yellow marbles.

'Remember when the babies grew up?' said Gem. 'They stayed in the nest while the parents went hunting. Then one started doing its own thing – it hopped away from the nest and flew to another tree. They split up for a while. But remember the last time we saw them?'

It was a warm November night, the promise of summer in the air. We had sat on the grass outside Gem's back door. Mum and Ben were there too. For a moment, we'd all stopped talking, as stars appeared above the neighbours' trees, like candles in the sky. We heard a low grunting call and then we saw them: the two young tawnies huddled together on the fence.

CHAPTER 29

Barn Owl

After Scrabble, Gem's ute spluttered off into the night and Mum helped me set up the daybed so I could sleep on the verandah.

'Looking for night birds?' She threw a blanket over my legs.

'Maybe.'

'Gem's story didn't cheer you up?'

I shrugged. Sure, Ben and I might hang out again one day, but that didn't help me now. Without Maggie, I felt more lost than ever. Worse than any vagrant.

Mum sat on the bed. I shuffled my legs over to give her room.

'I've got a bird story for you now.' She tied back her hair. 'Whenever I feel down and want to give up, I think of Maggie.'

'Really?'

'Yep. I think about how she was just flying along one day, minding her own business, when some big monster with four wheels knocked her to the ground. She should have died, Luke. But she didn't. She woke up the next day, sang a little song and kept on living.' The light from the kitchen coloured the side of her face and I thought of Ben, when he'd carried Maggie back to the house that night. 'So I think, if Maggie can scrape herself up and get on with life, then I can too.'

I didn't know Mum ever thought about stuff like that. It was like she'd opened her eyes to birds as well.

'Is that how you stopped being angry at Dad?'

'Sort of. The yoga and muffins helped too.' She held my hand. 'I don't know if Maggie'll ever come back, love. But don't give up on her. Or anything else.'

She kissed my head and said goodnight.

Just as she was about to stand up, something white flashed past the railing. It was a barn owl, barely there for a second before melting away into the night.

'Seen one of them before?' said Mum.

I shook my head, wide-eyed.

She gave me her half-smile. 'Told you not to give up.'

CHAPTER 30

The Dead of Night

I woke on the verandah in the middle of the night. Blinked into the empty black, darker than the deepest parts of the creek. A door squeaked, then the soft patter of feet on timber as somebody tiptoed down the front steps, on the other side of the house. I crept to the railing just in time to see Ben wheel his bike down the driveway and pedal off into the night, his footy bag strapped to his back.

I sat on the bed. My blood pounded in my ears. He said he wasn't going to steal the boat. Yelled and slammed the door in my face. Now he was sneaking out in the dead of night.

I shoved my arms into the sleeves of my jacket, ran down the steps and grabbed my bike. I pumped my feet on the pedals and followed him, slicing through the cold air like a boat, something fast – a yacht skimming the Pacific, ocean winds filling my sails.

His silhouette was just ahead of me. I slowed down to keep my distance. Eventually, he steered into a clumpy dirt lane that ran to the creek. I followed, keeping to the shadows. His tyres bumped along the gravel towards the trees at the end of the lane. Then he rode straight in, both Ben and bike dissolving into the darkness of the scrub.

I got off mine and stared at the spot where he'd gone in. It was mainly bush here and just a few houses. They looked like shapes cut from black cardboard, like the backdrop of a play. A mango tree rustled with flying foxes and a masked lapwing shrieked its night call, an eerie scream that echoed through the streets.

masked lapwing

I walked with my bike into the opening between the trees, along a narrow track. The night folded over me as leaves brushed my face and arms. Then I saw him through the mess of bush. He marched through the dark like he'd been here at night a hundred times before. I dropped my bike and ran after him, trying to skip silently over stones so he wouldn't hear me. The path opened in front of him and he headed straight to the old white boat. It stood out like a lighted window in a dark building.

'Ben! Don't!' I ran at him.

He spun around. 'Luke?'

I tackled him to the ground, wrestled, punched his chest. 'You lied!'

He pushed me off, then pinned me down in the dirt. 'Shush!' he hissed. 'What the hell are you doing?'

I wriggled under his weight, but couldn't move. 'You lied. You said you weren't gonna steal it.'

He brought his face close to mine until all I could see were his dark eyes. 'I'm not stealing anything,' he growled.

'Then what are you doing?'

His fists dug into my shoulders and held me down. Then he pushed himself off, shrugged his footy bag to the ground and sat on the edge of the boat. I stood up and shook dead leaves from my hair.

'I can't tell you,' he said. 'You gotta trust me.'

'Stop saying that! You ditched the book. You're sneaking out at night. And you never tell me anything.'

He flinched, like I'd landed a blow, but he still didn't talk. It was like I'd hooked a huge barramundi and couldn't reel it in.

After a few deep breaths, he looked at me, defeated. 'Fine,' he said. 'I'll show you something. But you're not gonna like it.'

CHAPTER 31

The Longest Tail

I followed him past the Jumping Tree, then we veered off the track until he found a tall wooden fence. He reached for the top of the palings and pulled himself up. In a second he was over, his feet scuffing the ground on the other side. I did the same, but grazed my arm on the wood and fell hard on my ankle when I landed.

My spine chilled. We were in a stranger's yard in the middle of the night. Neat grass, garden beds, and an old timber house like ours. Whose world had we broken into?

He dragged me by the sleeve to the back corner of the yard and stood me in front of a

cage, as big as a small shed, covered with a thick canvas sheet. There was the sweet smell of seed, a bit like the food we gave the chooks. Something shuffled inside.

I folded back the sheet. Nothing at first, then a shape moved near the top.

I held my breath. The shape moved again, then it edged onto a wooden perch and into the moonlight.

It was the bird I'd been searching for. The desert bird with a soft, scratchy call. Even in the dark, I could see the colours: pink chin, bright green wings, dusky blue head. And the longest tail I'd ever seen, twice as long as the bird itself.

'Princess parrot,' I whispered. It was beautiful. But it wasn't a vagrant. Vagrants were lost, unexpected visitors thrown off course. This bird was trapped.

I turned to Ben. 'You knew it was here?'

He stared at the bird and nodded.

'For how long?'

He shrugged.

'But ... whose place is this?'

Suddenly, a light snapped on behind us and we spun around.

'It's mine.' Frankie stood with a torch in her hand.

My head throbbed. Frankie's place? I never knew which house was hers because Ben had kept it to himself, until now.

'This is yours?' I pointed at the bird but kept my eyes on Frankie.

'It's my dad's.'

'This is the one I was looking for.' I couldn't keep still. 'You knew the whole time. Both of you!'

Frankie lowered the torch. 'We knew you'd hate it being trapped in a cage. I hate it too. That's why we didn't want you to find it.'

'Whatever.'

'It's true,' said Ben.

I rubbed the back of my neck and remembered the things Frankie had said. *Just a bird. Not gonna find it.* I thought she'd been teasing me the whole time. 'Are you serious? That's why you stopped me finding it?'

'Trust me.' Ben used his Dad voice.

Frankie shone the torch on the parrot.

I pictured page 176 of my bird guide and the small dot in the middle of the Australian map that showed where they were supposed to live. Dry, thirsty land. Spinifex grass and ghost gums, far away from Cabbage Tree Creek. I peered at the parrot's beady eye and wondered what it thought of this place, this cage. Wondered how it felt to have its wings clipped so it could hardly fly, to be a wild bird turned tame.

'You're right,' I said. 'I hate it.'

I walked back across the yard and reached for the top of the fence and dragged myself over. Left Ben behind. I didn't care, just wanted to find my bike and go home.

'Luke, wait!' Frankie landed on the ground behind me. 'I'm really sorry. I reckon it's cool how much you know about birds.'

'You called me Bird Nerd.'

She pulled a guilty face. 'Sorry. I didn't mean it.'

Then the fence creaked and we turned around. Ben jumped from the palings and hit the dirt. He stood, holding something to his chest, something that moved. A heaviness like a ship's anchor sank in my gut as I saw – it was the princess parrot.

He lifted it high in front of him, like a prize. It flapped a few times.

'Ben!' I screamed. 'What are you doing?'

He didn't answer. The parrot flapped again and this time he let go. It swooped low above our heads and flew away.

CHAPTER 32

Split Up

'What have you done?' I cried.

Ben scowled. 'I let it go. That's what you wanted.'

'No, it's not!' I pushed his chest and he stumbled.

'What's your problem? It's free!'

'It's a pet!' I yelled in his face. 'It won't survive out here.'

That shut him up.

Frankie was quiet too. She crouched and her face was as white as the old boat. 'My dad's gonna flip out.'

Ben scrunched his hair up in his hands.

His eyes were huge. My whole life, he'd always been in charge, always in control. But now it was up to me.

'Let's split up,' I said, my voice wobbly. 'It can't fly far.'

Ben took off, back along the track towards the boat. Frankie headed to the creek and I ran through the bush behind the houses. I scraped past hedges and branches, kicking rocks and snapping twigs under my feet. Then I stopped. Too much noise. I slowed my breathing and stood as still as the trees. Remembered what Gem said. *Pick a spot. The birds will come.* I listened to the quiet of the night. Waited for the parrot to call. I closed my eyes and sank into the silence, trying to hear something inside the emptiness.

And I did. Not a bird call, but something dragging along the dirt. Footsteps far away. Then a sound that nearly stopped my heart: the slap of timber hitting water.

Ben had taken the boat.

CHAPTER 33

All Birds at Once

By the time I made it to the creek, the boat was almost halfway across. Ben shoved a paddle through the water, churning the surface into a frothy mess.

'He saw the bird on the other side,' Frankie said, out of breath.

'Ben!' I cupped my hands round my mouth. 'It's gonna sink!'

'What?'

'The boat!' I shouted. 'It's gonna sink!'

He paused and the whole night seemed to freeze with him. His eyes swept over the boat. 'It's fine!'

He pushed the paddle back through the water. Maybe he was right and Mr Knight was wrong. It might not sink. I scanned the banks on the other side, trying to spot the parrot. Silhouettes and shadows but no bird.

Frankie tugged my sleeve and pointed at Ben. 'Look!'

The boat was sinking. It was hard to see through all the splashing, but it was slowly dipping lower. He didn't know. Just kept smashing the paddle through the water.

'Ben!' I screamed. 'It's sinking!'

He stopped and looked at me, confused. Then he looked down at the belly of the boat and echoed my cry. 'It's sinking!'

He dropped to his knees and scooped water out with his hands. I ran into the creek, crashed in the shallows and fell over. Frankie chased after me and dragged me back a few steps.

'Don't swim out,' she said. 'That's not gonna help.'

I scrambled back to the bank and watched him. He was hunched down, shovelling handfuls of water over the side. The boat edged lower.

'Just come back!' I yelled.

He stopped bailing. 'What?'

'Come back!'

He grabbed the paddle and drove it through the water. He didn't move anywhere except down. If he jumped out and let the boat drown, he'd be in huge trouble. From Mum. Mr Knight. Maybe the police again.

I had to think, but my body didn't make sense: I bounced on my toes, pulled at my hair, whacked the paperbark tree beside me. I stopped for a second, then placed my hand on the tree and looked up. It was the Jumping Tree. My eyes fell on the coiled-up rope, the one I used to swing into the creek. An idea hit me, but I didn't know if I could do it.

'Luke!' His voice was desperate. The boat was half-gone. 'Do something!'

I unhooked the rope and started to climb. Dragged myself up and crawled along the thick branch where Ben always jumped. I untied the other end of the rope and held the whole length in my hands. I crouched, rope in hand, poised to jump. But I couldn't do it. Just like last time, the whole world wobbled and shook. My chest hammered and my fingernails dug into the paperbark. This was something Ben could do. Not me.

'Help, Lukey!'

I lifted my head and looked straight at my brother. He stood frozen, holding the paddle, water up to his shins. I'd never seen him in trouble like this. All our lives, he'd propped me up. Rode with me to school, stuck up for me and tackled me off the road to save my life. Now, for once, he needed *me* to help. I had to jump.

His voice called across the creek. 'You can do it, Luke! Trust me.'

I closed my eyes, whispered down from three and sprang off the branch. For the smallest moment, I was all birds at once. A brown thornbill. Brahminy kite. A powerful owl on silent wings.

Then I fell. Plummeted into the night-black creek, sank deep in the watery dark. My body rushed back up to the surface and broke through. I gulped salty air and coughed, then swam out to Ben. Most of the boat was gone, so I threw him one end of the rope.

brahminy kite

'Tie it on!' I yelled. 'We'll drag it out.'

He knotted the rope to the boat and jumped over the side into the water, just as the whole thing went under. 'Let's go,' he gasped.

Frankie met us in the water. We swam to the bank, Frankie and me holding the rope, Ben with the paddle. Standing on the mud, we leant back and pulled on the rope. We slipped and fell and swore, but we pulled until we felt the weight coming towards us, like we were heaving a chest of gold to shore. Finally, the nose of the boat poked through the surface, then the whole thing reached the shallows. With a few grunts and trips, we dragged it onto the bank, then collapsed on the mud. Water spilt out through the cracks in the boat and at last, it was empty again. Just an old white boat resting on the edge of Cabbage Tree Creek.

I looked at the others. We were soaked and caked in filth, but we all smiled. Everything felt lighter, like the dirty creek had washed us clean.

'Now I know why nobody uses it,' joked Ben. 'Did you know it would sink?'

'Yeah,' I said. 'But you told me you weren't gonna take it.'

'I wasn't! But the bird was over—'

Then we saw it. The dark shape of the princess parrot swept across the creek and over our heads. Its long tail dragged behind like kite strings as it wove through the trees.

Ben knelt up. 'Looks like it's headed for your house, Frankie. Would it do that?'

'Hope so.' She craned her neck to follow its path. 'Probably knows it's safe there.'

'So all of that was for nothing,' he laughed, flopping back in the mud.

'Not really.' I whacked his arm. 'You got to take the boat out.'

He slipped me a look. 'And you jumped out of the tree.'

A Ben thing to do, I thought. A Luke thing too.

We pulled each other upright and dragged the boat up the grass, along the track, and tied it to the same old fence post in Mr Knight's yard. Ben grabbed his footy bag and we walked to Frankie's house to check on the bird. It was back in the cage, perched in the moonlight, as if nothing had happened. Frankie latched the cage and draped the sheet over. Ben and I climbed back over the fence and found our bikes. As we rode clear of the trees and onto the dirt road, the edges of the sky lightened, black smudging into blue. Morning was on its way.

CHAPTER 34

No Hands

We rode home in the strange early light. On the way, Ben told me everything he knew about the princess parrot, how it was Frankie's idea to hide it from me so I wouldn't get upset.

'It wasn't easy,' he said. 'You were desperate to find it.'

'Yeah. I had this weird idea.'

'What?'

I rested a hand on my knee as I rode, closed my eyes for a few seconds, opened them again. 'I thought we had a connection, the bird and me. Like we were both lost and out of place.'

Ben stopped pedalling and let the rolling

wheels carry him along the road. There was just enough light to see his dark eyes lock onto mine.

'You're not lost, Lukey. You're right here with me. We're apostlebirds, remember?'

I kept it going. 'Because we stick together?'

'Course not. Because we're ugly.'

We both laughed. I let go of the handlebars and rode no hands. But not too fast. Not a yacht on the ocean. More like a fishing canoe, drifting down the creek.

We parked our bikes under the house as the first kookaburra cleared its throat with a few low cackles. Ben climbed the steps in front of me and I grabbed his footy bag to stop him. I still didn't know what was in it.

'So why did you go out tonight, if you weren't gonna steal the boat?'

He grinned. 'Can't say. You gotta trust me.'

I shook my head, breathed a laugh, but didn't argue.

'And you have to do something else,' he said.

I followed him up the stairs. We tiptoed

across the floorboards and he led me to his room. He grabbed a book from under his bed and shoved it into my hands. *The Birds of Cabbage Tree Creek*.

'Finish it,' he said.

I crept to my room and collapsed on the bed, clutching the book. Ben must have grabbed it when I flung it into the bush. Like a weary seabird sinking through the sky and into its nest, a realisation settled warmly in my thoughts. Other kids were doing cool stuff and a book of birds probably wouldn't win, but Ben cared enough to save it. He didn't think it was stupid – he just didn't want me to find that caged bird.

CHAPTER 35

A Movie in Reverse

The sun poured through my window and hit me like a spotlight. I sat up in bed, rubbed my eyes and yawned. I'd never slept so late and the whole night felt like a year ago. Images filtered back into my head, starting from the end, like a movie in reverse. I remembered the bike ride home in the half-light, the swooping parrot, water spitting through the cracks of the boat. Further back I pictured Frankie's yard and the birdcage, tackling Ben and the moment I saw him sneaking off on his bike.

My mind rewound further until my stomach sank. Maggie. She was still gone and I'd lost count of the days. I drew her shape in my head. The strong beak, knee-length trousers and the whole world swimming in that dark brown eye.

Then some smaller things bubbled up in my memory. Gem's story about the tawnies, and the barn owl flying past the verandah. I thought of the way Ben and I had laughed on the ride home and when he told me I wasn't lost.

I slipped out of bed and stepped on something. It was *The Birds of Cabbage Tree Creek*. I remembered the last thing Ben had said. *Finish it*. I found a pencil, my binoculars, and took the book outside. I stood in the backyard and closed my eyes. Rosellas chirped. Pigeons cooed. A pied butcherbird sang my favourite call.

Things don't always work out. Maggie might not come back. But where there were birds, there was hope.

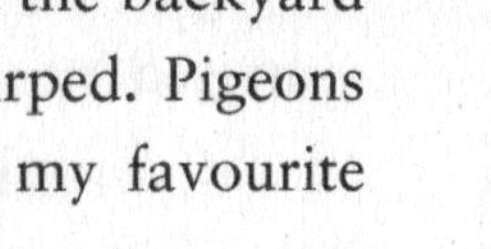

wonga pigeon

CHAPTER 36

A Beautiful Book

The ute windows were open as Gem and I puttered into town. She sang along to the radio at the top of her voice, a song about driving cars. The sounds of the suburb rose and fell as we drove: a leaf blower, kids squealing on a trampoline, somebody revving a car in their driveway. The wind flicked Gem's fiery crest of hair, like tiny flames dancing on her head. I still hadn't seen Maggie, but a ride in the ute always lifted me, at least a bit.

'Think you'll win, Lukey Luke?'

'No way,' I said. 'Hopefully I won't come last, though.'

The competition winners were being announced at the big park in town. Important people from the council would be there, as well as the seniors' choir that was always in the local paper. Gem offered to take me, and Mum was bringing Ben in her car.

The park was full of people, mingling and talking and laughing. Huge flags and banners flapped above our heads, each with a picture connected to the creek – a paperbark or a wooden jetty. Gem and I wriggled through the crowd to where a microphone waited in its stand on a small wooden platform. The choir performed next to the little stage, singing an old song about packing up your troubles. Their voices were high and wobbly and their faces were stretched into permanent smiles. On the other side of the stage was the fishing canoe, draped in shiny red ribbon. It was perfect.

A few kids from school waited with me. We talked about who might win and a girl called Violet seemed to know everything about the other entries.

'Sophie's not doing the play anymore,' she said. 'The family weren't very good actors and

she stormed out of rehearsals. And Bertie gave up his newspaper stories. Couldn't meet the deadline.'

This was good news for the rest of us. 'What about Willow and her paintings?' I said.

'Oh, yeah. She's still in it.'

'And the high school kids?'

'They lost interest,' said Violet. 'Mum said that's what teenagers do.'

The choir belted out its final notes and a tall man with a friendly round face tapped the microphone. He talked for a while, but I didn't really listen. Gem and I had spotted a crimson rosella in one of the park's giant fig trees. After a few minutes, Mum, Ben and Frankie found us. Mum squeezed my shoulders and Ben rested his elbow on my head.

The round-faced man was replaced by a woman with short grey hair and a sparkly smile, like she'd stepped out of a television game show. She held a few envelopes in her hand.

'This is it, Lukey,' whispered Gem.

The sparkly woman opened the envelope for third place. She flashed her toothpaste smile and announced a name. It was mine.

The crowd cheered. Ben pushed me towards the stage. My hands trembled as I stood next to the sparkly woman. She held *The Birds of Cabbage Tree Creek* above her head and her voice fluttered and dipped as she spoke. 'This beautiful book shows off the birds of the creek like never before. Anyone who flips through these pages will have their eyes opened to the wonder of these creatures we take for granted, these birds of Cabbage Tree Creek.'

She shook my quivering hand, paused for a photo, then gave me a voucher to spend at one of the shops in the main street. I skipped back to the others. They hugged me and scruffed my hair.

'Sorry I didn't win,' I said to Ben.

He threw an arm over my shoulder. 'Doesn't matter.'

Soon, Willow was on stage. She had come second. Three of her paintings were displayed on easels beside the wooden platform. As the woman's voice streamed out of the speakers, I thought about how she had described *The Birds of Cabbage Tree Creek*. A beautiful book, she'd said. And everyone's eyes would be opened to birds. It wasn't a boat, but it felt pretty good.

Willow left the stage and it was time for the winner to be announced. Everyone went quiet. Kids next to me bounced on their toes. Even the birds seemed to hold their voices. The woman peeled open the envelope and unfolded the paper with a flourish and a flick. She put her mouth to the microphone and read the winner's name.

CHAPTER 37

Wide-eyed and Laughing

It was Ben. My brother Ben. He walked chest-first to the wooden platform, not trembling for a second. The crowd roared with applause, loud like a summer storm on a tin roof. I joined in but couldn't smile or frown. My face didn't know what to do.

The noise of the crowd faded and the sparkly woman spoke with that wavering voice again. 'The standard of competition was incredibly high but, ladies and gentlemen, boys and girls, nobody captured the essence of Cabbage Tree Creek quite like Ben.'

A huge blanket was suddenly whipped away,

unveiling a wall of framed photographs on the stage. All black and white, each at least half a metre tall. Every photo depicted the creek and I recognised them all. One frame showed the Jumping Tree arched over the water. There was the battered shape of Mr Knight's boat, shining in the moonlight. A picture of the evening stars strung above the creek, another of a tunnel of trees. There was even a photo of a white-bellied sea eagle perched at the tip of a dead branch. They were stunning – each picture a piece of the creek, a perfect balance of light and shade.

In the middle of the wall was a photograph twice as big as the others, the centrepiece of the exhibition. The photo showed a boy in mid-air, falling towards the water. His face beamed, wide-eyed and laughing, caught in a moment of joy. It was me. After I'd jumped to save the boat that night, I'd hurled myself off the Jumping Tree almost every day. I didn't know when Ben had taken the picture, but I loved it. Everyone around me did too.

The choir started singing again and Ben had his photo taken. We ran across and buried him in a group hug. Mum and Gem talked over each other while Ben and I grabbed the paddles and circled the boat. Frankie ran her hand along the shiny edge.

'Can't believe you won!' I swished a paddle through the air.

'You're not mad? That I won and you didn't?'

'No way.' I swung the paddle like a cricket bat and remembered the days I had been upset, when I thought he'd teased me or that he was almost a thief. But the memories had a new shape now, a different colour, like the gold that fell on the trees at sunset. He'd tried to keep me from the parrot so I wouldn't get upset. And he'd taken all those photos to win the boat.

'You kinda helped,' he said.

I screwed up my face. 'Me?'

'Yeah. When we looked for birds, it made me take notice of everything, the trees and the sky and all that stuff. I pictured everything like it was a photo.'

I knew what he meant. *When you open your eyes to birds, the world opens itself in return.* 'But where'd you get the camera?'

He and Frankie shared a look. 'That's why I couldn't tell you.' He kept his eyes down. 'It's yours.'

'What?'

'It's your camera. It's your present from Dad. I couldn't stand it sitting there in the lounge room all that time. So I opened it. Sorry.'

I gripped the paddle. I could have whacked him, hit him for six. But I was done being mad. There was no point keeping a present wrapped up, like a bird in a cage. 'That's what was in the footy bag all that time?'

'Yeah.'

'And when I heard you were gonna take something?'

'Just photos, Lukey.'

'So that's why you snuck out that night – to take photos?'

'Yep.'

I shrugged. 'In a weird kind of way, Dad's gonna help us get to The Pocket after all.'

He twirled the paddle and his eyes shone. 'And you can see all the birds you want. All over the creek.'

We said bye to Frankie and walked across

the park to the cars. Ben slapped me on the back. 'Where d'you wanna go first, Lukey?'

'Across to the other side. Find more birds. What about you?'

'Straight to The Pocket. Catch a boat full of fish.' He dropped his arm over my shoulder. 'Then we'll follow the creek as far as it goes.'

Before we reached the car, we stopped. Dad stood not far away, about the length of a cricket pitch. He scratched the back of his head and he looked nothing like a powerful owl.

Ben strolled over. Dad patted his shoulder, shook his hand and said a few things I couldn't hear. Then he waved at me. Held his hand in the air and waited. This time I didn't run away. I had to grow up. So I waved back.

CHAPTER 38

Apostlebirds

That afternoon, Frankie came over and we celebrated on the verandah with homemade pizza. Mum and Gem piled olives and salami on theirs. Frankie and I shared one, a tower of tomato and cheese. Ben had a meaty one all to himself.

The sun had almost gone. I zipped up my jacket and lifted the collar around my neck. Mum reckoned the autumn winds blew in from the bay and followed the creek straight to our verandah. At least it drove the sandflies away. Ben told us about his secret photo shoots to get the pictures of the creek, taking off at dawn and sneaking out at night. I chewed my pizza and listened, but I was all mixed up inside. The boat was ours, but the poinciana was still empty. It had been ages without Maggie and I didn't know if I'd ever see her again.

Gem caught my eye. She tapped the table for attention and made her voice brighter than usual. 'Okay, Luke and I play this game called Soul Bird.'

I gave her a screwed-up smile. 'You need a better name.'

She rolled her eyes. 'Anyway, if you were a bird, what would you be? I'd be a scarlet honeyeater.'

'Ooh, a willie wagtail,' said Frankie. 'I love those birds.'

'Great!' Gem gave one loud clap and turned to Mum. 'What about you? What would you be?'

Mum bit the edge of a pizza crust, chewed for a while and swallowed. 'Some kind of cuckoo, so I could dump my kids with someone else and fly away.'

We cracked up laughing and Gem's cockatoo cackle drowned us out.

Mum raised her eyebrows. 'And what bird would you be, Luke?'

I buried my hands in my pockets. 'Brown thornbill.'

'What's that look like?'

'Here,' said Gem. She grabbed my bird guide from the daybed and opened to the page of thornbills, small unremarkable birds clinging to twigs.

Mum eyed the page. 'I get it,' she said. 'It looks plain, but it's not really. Bit of orange on the head, light brown stripes, yellow underneath. Nice rusty colour on the tail, and check out that blood-red eye. There's more to it than you think. It suits you, love.'

I shivered a bit from the cold, but Mum's words sent a little buzz through my bones.

Gem turned to Ben. 'That just leaves you.'

Frankie shoved his shoulder. 'He's a bird of paradise, always showing off.'

'Wedge-tailed eagle,' I said. 'Biggest bird of prey.'

Ben screwed his nose up. 'I'm none of those,' he said. 'And Luke's not a thornbill either. We're the same bird, remember, Lukey?'

I met his grin. 'Apostlebirds.'

'Yep.'

'Because we're ugly.' I laughed.

'Nah,' he said. 'Not because we're ugly.'

I suddenly didn't feel cold anymore. Those few words from Ben had given me an idea.

CHAPTER 39

A Useless and Important Thing

A couple of days later, I stuck Ben's apostlebird drawing on the back wall of the classroom. He never knew I'd kept it after he threw it under his bed that day, but I'd unscrunched it and kept it flattened between some books on my desk, sometimes stealing a look at it. Even though I hadn't drawn it, it was perfect for the class wall: useless to everyone else, but important to me.

When I told Mr Knight about it, his eyes and moustache smiled together.

CHAPTER 40

Two Boys (and Sometimes a Girl) in a Boat

'Paddle, Lukey! Paddle!'

We were on the water for the first time. Ben shouted orders from the back of the canoe. I sat at the front, digging the paddle into the creek, pushing back, churning up the brown water.

'That's it! Keep going!'

All I could see was frothy water exploding all around me. My arms burnt and my eyes stung. I choked for air. Then I stopped and turned around. Ben lazed back with his hands behind his head. The paddle lay across his chest.

'Are. You. Even—' I coughed a few times. 'Are you even *paddling*?'

Ben straightened up, like I'd woken him from a nap. 'Oh, yeah,' he said, fake yawning. 'I did for a bit. But you were doing such a good job, I thought I'd relax and let you do all the work.'

I bent forward on my arms and laughed air back into my chest.

'Go on, then,' he said. 'Keep going.'

I swung around and scooped a paddleful of water into his face. That really woke him up. He grabbed his paddle and heaved water straight at me. It slapped me in the back and soaked my shorts. Then we both went for it, sweeping water onto each other, a splashing frenzy in the middle of the creek, until a voice cut through the noise.

'Hey!' We stopped. It was Mum. She stood on the bank, hands high on her hips, face like a thundercloud rolling in from the west. 'You boys going to row that thing? I'm trying to take a photo!'

So we paddled and it didn't take long to get used to it. Ben steered from the back, I kept us moving in the front. On that first day, we coasted to the Jumping Tree, then explored a thin

arm of the creek that led to a small sandy bank, almost like a beach. We spotted some friarbirds, a sacred kingfisher and a dollarbird.

'Good camping spot,' he said. 'Imagine waking up here.'

'Just us and the birds,' I said.

We spent every weekend in the boat, doing all the things we'd talked about. Caught bucketloads of fish at The Pocket. Camped under the stars. Even followed the creek as far as it went, where we caught sight of the mouth emptying into the bay. Sometimes Frankie squashed in too. She and Ben took photos while I watched the world through my binoculars, adding to *The Birds of Cabbage Tree Creek*. Sometimes I caught a flash of black and white through the trees. I never knew if it was Maggie or another magpie. But I reckon Maggie would have come over, if it was her.

I missed her song in the mornings and her cheeky gargling sounds when she met me in the afternoons. I missed watching her strut on the grass, listening for worms in the dirt.

But I thought about her most whenever we hosed down the boat because her name was painted along the side.

CHAPTER 41

My Brother, the Bird

It happened months later, at the start of spring. I was slouched on the daybed as the morning fog thinned, like the last chill of winter melting away. Stripes of sunlight reached the verandah and a blue-faced honeyeater announced the new day. I loved this time, when no-one else was awake. I had the whole planet to myself.

Suddenly, she appeared, swooped up and landed on the railing. She stood tall, beak angled up, sun on her back. She shook her feathers, then tilted her head and looked straight at me with that chocolate-brown eye. I blinked and sat forward.

'Maggie?' She bounced onto the daybed, edged closer and let me stroke the back of her neck. My fingers were shaking. 'Where've you been?'

She hopped back onto the railing and gargled her throaty little song. Then she flapped down to the grass and snapped a bug in her beak.

'Nice one, Mag!'

She swept up to the poinciana tree and landed beside another magpie. It was smaller, grey and white, just like Maggie was when we found her. The younger one squawked and she dropped the bug into its beak.

I ran inside and dragged Mum and Ben out of bed. As we reached the railing, Maggie threw back her head and sang to the morning sky. The younger magpie joined in, their melodies overlapping.

'She's a mum,' said Ben. 'All grown up.'

Mum wrapped her arms around me.

Later that day, Ben and I were out on the creek. The trees were filled with birdsong, new families welcoming the season. The front of the boat sliced through the water. Our fishing rods hung over the edge.

'Where do you think she went?' He pushed his paddle slowly, steering us around a shallow bend.

'Not sure. Anywhere, I guess. Had to find a mate.'

'Yeah,' he said. 'Maybe there's no handsome magpies around here.'

We ducked under a low branch reaching over the water.

'Do you think she'll stay?' he said.

I didn't know. Hadn't expected her to leave in the first place. 'Hope so.'

'And what about Dad?'

'I don't think he's coming back.'

'I know,' said Ben. 'I mean – are you gonna see him?'

I spotted Maggie halfway up a gum tree. During the time she'd been gone, I'd talked to Dad on the phone a bit. 'Yeah. When he's here next month. Might go to The Pocket.'

We rounded the boat into a wide stretch of the creek, the size of half a football field. We stopped paddling.

'Lukey, swap for a second.'

'Hey?'

'Swap places. I wanna do something.'

I shuffled to the back of the canoe and he climbed over me to the front. He rested his paddle next to the rods and pulled off his shirt. The boat wobbled as he stood. Then he took a big step forward and balanced on the very tip. I clenched my hands on the sides of the boat. He raised his arms wide, took a breath and jumped. Against the faded background of trees and blue sky, my brother was a bird. A wedge-tailed eagle. Bird of paradise. An ugly apostlebird leaping from a branch.

He plunged into the water and waves rocked the boat. Then he burst back up through the surface, laughing and punching the water at me. I paddled a bit closer and he climbed and fell back in the boat.

I loved it when Ben did things like that. And no wonder I thought he was a bird.

There was nothing I loved more.

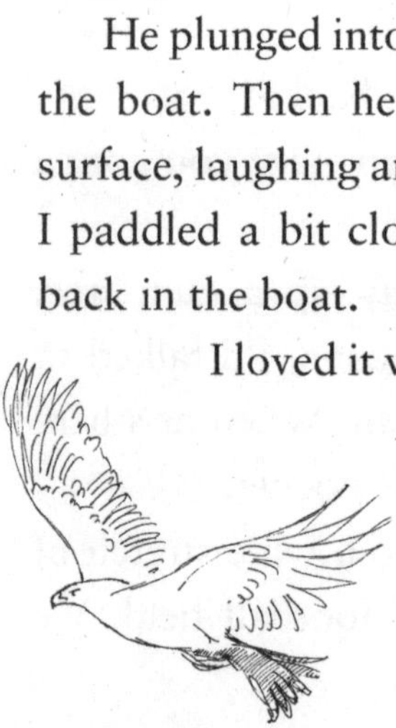

wedge-tailed eagle

In memory of Mum

AUTHOR NOTES

Cabbage Tree Creek

My mother grew up in Deagon, Brisbane, with a backyard that rolled into Cabbage Tree Creek. This inspired the setting for the story but the description of Luke and Ben's creek doesn't always match the original creek. I made some changes for narrative purposes, and my own memories of growing up near Currimundi Lake played a part too. I kept the name 'Cabbage Tree Creek' as a tribute to Mum and because I like how it sounds.

Birds

I've done my best to include birds that normally live around this creek, the surrounding suburbs or not too far away.

ACKNOWLEDGEMENTS

The idea for this story may have hatched in my mind, but many other people taught it to fly. Thank you to the following:

Clair Hume for being positive from the start, bashing the early drafts into shape and cheering me all the way to the end.

Cathy Vallance for an outstanding editor's eye and for helping me overcome my addiction to commas.

Mark Macleod for lifting the story with an edit that was detailed, honest and caring.

Jo Hunt for a wonderful design and for assembling a beautiful cover from my raw ingredients.

The whole team at UQP for supporting my work.

Morris Gleitzman, Meg McKinlay, Karen Foxlee and Glenda Millard for sharing such kind words about the story.

Mum, Dad, Tom, Jo and Mike (and families) for unwavering support.

Michael Livingston for bird advice and friendship.

Finally, Bron, Sophie, Willow, Florence the dog and Harry the cat – thanks for putting up with me while I wrote another book and for filling my days with love and laughs.

Peter Carnavas writes and illustrates books for children. He has made many picture books, such as *The Children Who Loved Books*, *Last Tree in the City* and *A Quiet Girl*. His novel *The Elephant* won a Queensland Literary Award and was shortlisted in four other national awards. He has won an Australian Book Industry Award and a SCBWI Crystal Kite Award, and his books have been published widely across the world. Peter lives on the Sunshine Coast, Queensland, with his wife, two daughters, a dog and a cat.

www.petercarnavas.com

First published 2021 by University of Queensland Press
PO Box 6042, St Lucia, Queensland 4067 Australia
Reprinted 2022, 2024

uqp.com.au
reception@uqp.com.au

University of Queensland Press (UQP) acknowledges the Traditional Owners and their custodianship of the lands on which UQP operates. We pay our respects to their Ancestors and their descendants, who continue cultural and spiritual connections to Country. We recognise their valuable contributions to Australian and global society.

Cover and internal illustrations by Peter Carnavas
Cover design by Jo Hunt
Typeset in 11.5/17 Sabon LT Pro by Post Pre-press Group, Brisbane
Printed in Australia by McPherson's Printing Group

Queensland Government

University of Queensland Press is supported by the Queensland Government through Arts Queensland.

Australian Government | Australia Council for the Arts

University of Queensland Press is assisted by the Australian Government through the Australia Council, its arts funding and advisory body.

A catalogue record for this book is available from the National Library of Australia.

ISBN 978 0 7022 6333 0 (pbk)
ISBN 978 0 7022 6528 0 (epdf)
ISBN 978 0 7022 6529 7 (epub)
ISBN 978 0 7022 6530 3 (kindle)

University of Queensland Press uses papers that are natural, renewable and recyclable products made from wood grown in well-managed forests and other controlled sources. The logging and manufacturing processes conform to the environmental regulations of the country of origin.

MIX
Paper | Supporting responsible forestry
FSC® C001695
FSC www.fsc.org

Also by Peter Carnavas
THE ELEPHANT

Winner – Queensland Literary Awards
Shortlisted – NSW Premier's Literary Awards
Shortlisted – CBCA Book of the Year Awards
Shortlisted – Australian Book Industry Awards

Olive's father has a sadness so big that she imagines it as an enormous elephant following him around. Every day Olive sees the elephant, and every day she wishes it would go.

With the help of Grandad and her best friend, Arthur, Olive sets out to chase the elephant away.

But how can Olive move something so big?

Beautifully written, this novel from acclaimed author and illustrator Peter Carnavas will stay with you long after reading.

'*The Elephant* is a timeless and memorable tale that will deeply move and delight readers of all ages.'
Oz Books 4 Teachers

'This book is a rare treasure.' ***Bookity Boo* blog**

'Lovingly illustrated ... beautifully told.' **Youth Services Book Review**

ISBN 978 0 7022 5961 6

UQP